The Homeschool Reader

Collected Articles from
Home Education Magazine
1984-1994

The Homeschool Reader

Collected Articles from
Home Education Magazine
1984-1994

From the Editors of Home Education Magazine

The Homeschool Reader

edited by Mark and Helen Hegener

Published by
Home Education Magazine
Post Office Box 1083
Tonasket, WA 98855
(509) 486-1351
Orders@homeedmag.com
http://www.homeedmag.com

First printing 1988.
Second printing 1990.
Revised printing 1993.
Second Revised edition 1995.
Second Revised edition, updated 1997.
Third Revised edition 2006.
Printed in the United States of America.

ISBN 0-945097-30-1

Library of Congress Cataloging-in-Publication Data

Hegener, Mark and Helen
   The Homeschool Reader, Third Revised Edition

   Includes index.
   1. Home schooling. 2. Hegener, Helen, 1950-.
   II. Title.
   LC40.H44   2006   370.19'3   88-32018
   ISBN 0-945097-30-1   2005938796

Acknowledgements

We'd like to express our sincere appreciation to the many contributors to this third edition, and to Holt Associates, of Cambridge, Massachusetts, for permission to reprint the writings of John Holt. We'd also like to extend our appreciation to the inimitable Sue Patch for shepherding this third edition into print.

Dedication

As always, this one's for the kids who lovingly taught us what we needed to know: Michael, Christopher, Jody, Jim, and John.
We're still learning from you all.

Table of Contents

Part Three
Subjects One Two Three

Reading/Writing

Math/Science

History/Geography/Social Studies

Other Studies

Part Four
Advanced Learning

Part Five
Networking

Part Six
Personal Experiences

Appendixes

Index

Introduction to the 2006 Edition

Helen Hegener

We have a big red spiral-bound notebook, one of those 200 page, college ruled notebooks divided into five subject areas. Written across the cover in black marker are these words: *Home Education Magazine*, Issue 1, Volume 1 (putting it together). This notebook was literally the blueprint for the first issue of the magazine from which the articles in this book are taken.

Inside are notes such as this listing from the first page: bulk mail rates, licenses? permits? advertising - where and how - costs? printing - available options, need a title - cover? advertisers - how to obtain, what to charge, subscriptions - 12 issues, $20.00/year or $2.00/issue, welcome contributions - no pay yet. The date was 12-26-83. We'd never produced a magazine before, and we had a lot of questions about how it was done.

The next page is a listing of potential content: Editorial, Articles, Interviews, Resources and Reviews, Kids Korner, Homeschooling Hints, Directory, Legislative News, Letters, Questions and Answers, Local Support Group News. Interestingly, most of those features can still be found in today's *Home Education Magazine*.

On page after page the first content of the magazine is written out in longhand, in blue ink - in some places items are scribbled over and corrections or additions made. Editing was done later, in red ink - but there's little of that. It's amazing how much content went to print exactly as it was laid out in the notebook.

The first issue of *Home Education Magazine* was twenty pages long; ten double-sided sheets of paper stapled along the left-hand side. It featured an editorial, a couple of articles, an interview with a homeschooling family, reviews of several educational items, a book review, a report from the Washington Legislative Action Committee (which was a group of homeschooling parents who were working on a homeschooling bill to introduce to the Legislature), a few good quotes and a short listing of helpful homeschooling resources.

Looking at that big red notebook today, it's fascinating to consider that what was optimistically written there so long ago has morphed and grown into the premier magazine for homeschooling families today. And yet it seems somehow fitting, a hands-on indication that - like homeschooling itself - the magazine behind this book grew from a simple idea and the faith, hopes, trust and hard work of many people.

This third edition of *The Homeschool Reader*, encompassing the first ten years of *Home Education Magazine*, is the first in a new series of Readers we've planned for publication. As these books go into production over the coming months and years we'll be revisiting the history of the magazine time and again, rediscovering favorite articles and columns, marveling at how intertwined the magazine and its many contributors are with the history and the future of the homeschooling movement.

Adapted from an editorial which appeared in our Sept-Oct, 2005 issue.

Part One

HOMESCHOOLING

Why Homeschool?

Kathleen McCurdy

The question keeps coming up: Why do people want to home school? To the friends and relatives of the home schoolers it seems an eccentricity: school was good enough for them, why would you want to be so out of step with the world? To the sociologists and religionists it seems frightening: how will those children become socialized, conformed to the mores of the day? To the professional educator it is positively infuriating: how can an untrained person presume to take the intellectual training of a child into his own hands? And the neighbors wonder why anyone would want to have the children under foot all day...

So why are so many people deciding to pull their children out of school, or simply never send them in the first place? This question seems to elicit a variety of answers. There is a concern for the child's academic achievement: the gifted child who lacks stimulus at school, the late bloomer who needs more time to learn at his own rate. There are parents who want a certain philosophical or spiritual influence to permeate their child's learning experience. Some parents feel that just as they must protect their child from physical harm until he is able to look after himself, they are also responsible for protecting that child from the moral evils prevalent in today's society.

Though not usually mentioned at first, experienced home schoolers give yet another reason to home school: the joy of a child's company and of sharing with him the excitement of discovery and learning. I believe this last reason is the real heart of the home school movement. The discovery, or more properly, rediscovery, of the joys of parenting will assure the continued growth and persistence of the home school phenomenon. The attrition rate is not very great among this kind of home schooling family.

No doubt schools will learn to adapt to the needs of the consumer now that they have the need to do so. Parents who only home school for social, moral, or philosophical reasons will eventually find private schools to meet their needs, or may even get together and create their own cooperative schools. After all, bringing the school back home, keeping track of curriculum, hours, lessons, and grades is a pretty big order for parents who also have to earn a living or otherwise keep house and perhaps look after a preschooler as well.

The real home schoolers, the ones who are here to stay, are the ones who have come to understand the meaning of parenting. These parents have learned to resist the urge to "teach" their children (as in "teacher"). They have grown accustomed to expect that their children will learn because there is something to learn. Whatever it is that parents do in the course of their daily living that makes them successful and fulfilled human beings is what their children will learn. These parents will help, encourage, answer questions, share in the discoveries, and maybe even learn with their children. And they wouldn't give up this privilege for anything in the world!

Parents who send their children off to day care at two or three, and later enroll them in preschool and kindergarten, cannot understand what these home schoolers are talking about — and home schoolers find such "liberated" parents equally incomprehensible. But research shows that home schoolers have chosen a better way. Their children have better motor skills, social graces, and better reasoning powers. They have been liberated from enslavement to peer pressure. They are free to do and to be whatever is their destiny to become. These are the reasons for home schooling.

From the November, 1986 issue of *Home Education Magazine.*

Dear New Homeschooler

Mary McCarthy

Dear New Homeschooler,

First, welcome and congratulations on your decision to home-school.

So you've gone to the library and checked out all the books on homeschooling. That's good. Except after you've sat down and read them all you're more confused than before because no two "experts" agree on how to homeschool. Don't worry about it, you will be home-schooling your own children in your own way.

Don't be scared off by the ones that tell you how your children can grow up to be Nobel Prize winners. It's possible (anything is possible) but not probable. Your goal is happy, educated children who like learning.

Don't be scared off by the ones that tell you that you must have an impeccably clean house and be well organized. If that were so there would only be one or two homeschooling families in existence. Face it, with kids home all day - doing the most interesting things - a mess is inevitable; enjoy it!

Don't be scared off by the ones that tell you that a strict schedule is necessary and must be adhered to. Life isn't like that. It would be great if it were, but life is unpredictable. Enjoy the surprises. Think of them as opportunities.

Notice that the most stringent books are written by men. Now I'm no sexist, but if they're not doing the housekeeping, they ought to stick to whatever it is they do best.

Notice how many ordinary people have written books about their successful homeschooling program. They're just like you, having once stood in those same shaky shoes. that's what you should be getting out of all those books: That ordinary parents, just like you, can achieve success in homeschooling. Each one found little tricks and experiences that helped them, and may help you too. But the basic message is that they all succeeded.

So who am I with all this unsolicited advice? Just a Mom who's made Plenty of Mistakes in the last 15 years of homeschooling. Not to worry - I still have plenty to make, and so do you.

You will have doubts, plenty of them! Can I really educate my child? You taught them to walk and talk, dress and feed themselves, understand right from wrong. How much more difficult can ABC and 123 be? Look back - you've already done the tough stuff, and without a curriculum!

Support groups are not mandatory. If you're very fortunate you'll be able to locate a group near you that meets your needs. If not it's not the end of the world. You can still throw the kids in the car and head for the museum, aquarium, park Renaissance Festival or whatever. You could start your own group, or just go ahead and educate your kids without a group. Sometimes it's better for new homeschoolers to focus on the family at the beginning rather than trying to juggle a family and a group.

The next biggest challenge is deciding on a curriculum. You can

make it up as you go along with lots of help from the library or purchase a curriculum-in-a-box with everything from pencils to report
cards. Most new homeschoolers like the security of the curriculum-in-
a-box but also find it restrictive and, over time, hard to stick with the
regimentation it mandates. If you're typical, by March half of it will
be lost under the beds and in the garage. The kids will help you lose
the least interesting things in it. ("Oops! How did that get in the
trash?") Listen to them, it's their education and they are ready to run
with it.

Anything that requires tears (on anyone's part) isn't worth the
effort. Put it away for another day (or year). Learning is supposed to
be a lifelong enjoyable process. Try and figure out why it isn't working
and either experiment with a different way or drop it altogether.
Accept that none of us is overly proficient in everything. Nor are we
ready to learn something just because our curriculum guide says we
are. Maybe you don't have a rocket scientist there, just a very interesting little person who has ideas of their own about what's necessary to
learn. Three hours of tears and cajoling to accomplish one workbook
page of nouns does not teach nouns. It teaches "I hate workbook pages
of nouns." Try putting the workbook away and doing a couple of
books of "Mad-Libs." Much more fun!

What if you have five children all at different grade levels? First off,
throw away that grade level thing. It's a way of comparing children,
and in a home setting just isn't necessary. Then see if you can combine
several children in one subject. I've never seen it written anywhere that
children can't work together on learning. The added responsibility and
confidence that comes from having the older ones help the younger
ones is a more valuable lesson than any forgotten math. A large part
of home education is just learning to work with the flow, rather than
whatever you think it should be. Allow each child to pursue interests
on their own. You may have one that shows up at the same time every
day at the kitchen table ready to go and flies through lessons with very
little supervision. That gives you time to locate the one still running
around in their underwear and "blanky" with a book, hunting for the
cat so the book can be read under the proper circumstances. Each
child is different. It's just a matter of parents learning to respect and
encourage the individual.

Relatives! Unfortunately most of us have them. And most of them
thought we were strange long before we announced we'd decided to
homeschool the kids. Smile, be kind, and be firm in your commit-

ment to home education. Some just need to see the progress, others will think you're totally incompetent. Include them all. They often make good mentors, so don't be afraid to ask Grandpa to show Junior how he does something he's really good at. Hopefully Grandma will be flattered by your request to show the kids how to do something she's experienced at. The ones you can't win over, or those who snub you - well, there's not much you can do about the actions of some people so just accept them and get on with it. The trick - with all the relatives preying on your doubts - is not to lose your focus on the children and their education.

You will have those days. It's okay. Even if you weren't home-schooling they would happen. Recognize that not much is accomplished under those circumstances and don't force things. in spite of what you've been led to believe homeschooling parents are not perfect (trust me on this one). Life will occasionally hand you a disaster. I've noticed that in times of hardship some people will send their children back to school. But most homeschoolers include the children and pull together as a family.

Decompression is a homeschool term used to define the time between taking the children out of public or private education and when they start expressing an interest in their own education. Parents also go through this unsettling period, but it's normal, so don't panic or force the issue. The longer the child was in the formal education system the longer the decompression. For teens it can be a year of teeth-grinding, nerve-wracking aggravation for which you will be rewarded many times over. Promise.

Do you need to know every subject to "teach" (I hate that word!) your children? Absolutely not. If that were so I wouldn't look so blank when a son tries to explain computers or the hydraulics of a 747 or whatever to me. It's best to just learn along with them and to appear interested. Learn phrases like, "That's nice, dear," and "Did you do this all by yourself?" and "Do the neighbors know?" These will come in handy.

Ask stupid questions. It's important for the child to feel accomplished at different things. It's okay to ask a child for help - humbling, but okay.

Ignore the myths about supermoms. We've all heard the stories about those proud parents with life size replicas of the space shuttle in the backyard, but until you actually see one don't fret about your kid having only recently figured out how to wire a light bulb to a battery.

I think some parents tend to exaggerate.

There's a very strong tendency for new homeschoolers to jump in with both feet, eyes covered and try to do everything all at once. It's normal. We just want everything for our kids, but it leads to very early burnout. When you feel the strain starting to wear, back off. Take a month off and relax. Don't forget that you're a student at this too, and you deserve time for yourself. Your children will love you for it. If the kids are happy and interested in learning then you are doing this homeschooling thing right.

Before you know it you'll be sitting there watching the children learn all on their own and suddenly it will dawn on you that there wasn't anything like your homeschool program in any of the books you read. Congratulations! Now you're an expert!

From the January-February, 1994 issue of *Home Education Magazine*.

Home Education is for Amateurs

Earl Stevens

Parenthood remains the greatest single preserve of the amateur.
- Alvin Toffler

I'm glad that parenthood remains the preserve of the amateur. If it should ever become the exclusive territory of experts the world will be in even more trouble than it is now. Parenthood is something that must be embraced freshly by novices as an act of love, not learned by specialists as a career choice. As an amateur, I'm still learning how to be a parent, and I'm also learning about this adventure called "home education."

Though we use phrases with the words "education" and "schooling" in them to describe what we do, our commitment ideally goes far deeper than a focus upon the methods by which our children become acquainted with academics. Indeed, despite what we hear from school officials and some homeschooling specialists, many of us have discov-

ered that the academic aspect of homeschooling is easily and painlessly accomplished. We are amazed by our children and often feel that
what we learn from them is more profound than what they learn from
us.

But homeschooling doesn't always look so simple to the uninitiat-
ed. In our Southern Maine support group we frequently hear the
question, "How do I get started with homeschooling? What is the
best thing to do?" As seasoned homeschoolers, one of the worst things
we can do is to answer the question precisely. It is better for a support
group to say to a prospective homeschooling parent, "We have wonderful news for you. Home education is a job for amateurs. Nobody
knows what you and your children should do. It is a deeply personal
adventure for each family and no two adventures are alike. We will
show you what we do and tell you what others do, but you will have
the satisfaction and delight of finding your own answers."

This news is not always welcome at first. The schools have told us
what to do with ourselves for many many years. They were the
experts, and even while we deny them our children it is sometimes difficult for us to give up the notion that we need to find still another,
more knowledgeable expert. We want very badly to do the right
thing for our children. We don't mind being amateur players, but we
wonder whether or not we understand the game sufficiently to be our
own managers. In our insecurity, it is tempting to seek and follow the
direction of an expert, even more so if our local support group is dedicated to his principles and methods. Finding our own answers can be
uncomfortable when neighboring homeschooling families, as well as
our friends and relatives, are wondering if we know what we are doing.

However there is no safety in expertise or in numbers. We find that
no matter how carefully we have planned, no matter what books we
have read or which experts we have consulted, our children don't easily fit into established patterns. Sometimes we can plainly see that in
spite of our hard work homeschooling isn't working academically. Or
perhaps the level of harmony and the overall happiness of the family
is beginning to ebb. Sometimes we simply begin to feel that there
must be more to life than this for our children and for ourselves.
Homeschooling can become a task and a trial, not the high adventure
we had expected.

The vision which at first seemed so bright and clear can become
muddy and confusing, and we are surrounded by conflicting advice
and struggles for our allegiance.

The experts in methodology fail us not because they always define childhood falsely but because they define it so much. Once we have labored to decide what all children are and what they should become we have lost sight of the children who stand before us. It is impossible to constantly compare a child to an ideal no matter how worthy and to see that child clearly at the same time. It is impossible to chase constantly after goals for our children and still be listening to them with profound attention.

While it may be a little scary at first, it is also exhilarating to discover that there are no prefabricated definitions and answers that can be uniformly applied to our homeschooling. This discovery allows us the freedom to search for our own solutions. It is at this point where parents often realize that what is necessary for them to succeed has always resided within themselves. The primary ingredient has to do with love and the attention born of love that came with parenthood and brought us to homeschooling in the first place.

Homeschooling is an act of liberation and an act of passion. It is an occasion to walk away from institutional images of life and to embrace a vision that is filled with personal meaning and unmistakable truths for our families. The quality of awareness that comes from the heart is more dependable and gets us into less trouble than does a determined loyalty to systems and procedures. We find that homeschooling is not about filling children with information and launching them into the workforce; it is about helping to make it possible for them to reach maturity with healthy, curious, fully conscious minds.

As parents there is one thing that we can all do very well for our children if only we allow ourselves opportunities. We can give them our complete attention. I don't mean the attention we give them when we take them to the zoo instead of cleaning the house, or the attention we give them when we are helping them become educated by whatever method is most pleasing to us, or the attention we give them under the heading of ethical guidance or religious instruction. I'm talking about the attention which comes when we look upon them with uncluttered minds, without goals and hidden agendas. When we see our children clearly we do what is appropriate; when we are unable to see them clearly we make silly mistakes. It is very difficult to see even what exists right before our eyes when our vision is clouded with ideals, strategies, and plans for the future.

Remember the clarity with which we see a new baby. A baby requires so much care, but we don't think about the care when we look at the baby. And we don't just *look* at the baby. We *see* the baby. We see the baby in a way that nourishes our spirit and guides our actions. There is nothing at all confusing about relating to a baby. It is not always so simple to see the child who has been with us for many years and who has grown into a more complex and less physically dependent person. Life has had many opportunities to distort our vision and divide our attention. Sometimes, in order to see the child, it helps to remember the baby.

We spend so much time preparing our children for the future that we tend to live in the future instead of the present. The education specialists are experts on the future, and they have devised all sorts of methods by which we can guide our children to competency and happiness. But I find that I am farthest from my child when I am busy being the leader, the guide, and the fortune teller. When suddenly I realize that this is happening to me I remember the baby. Then, at least for a while, I remember to just let myself be with the child and to trust that as I see him clearly I will respond to him wisely.

A homeschooling mother in Canada recently sent a letter to me which ended with a quote by Roque Dalton, "May we keep hauling up the morning." I like the metaphor of sailing a ship upon the sea for parenthood and for homeschooling. There are no completely reliable charts, and so we must often navigate without them. We must learn for ourselves how to find the currents, avoid the reefs and storms, and enter the harbors. As we haul up sails to go on sailing, so we haul up the morning for the adventures of each successive day. There is room for everybody on this ocean, and there is no pilot's license required or worth having. We must trust ourselves and our children. May each of us keep hauling up the morning.

From the September-October, 1990 issue of *Home Education Magazine*.

Homeschooling is for Everyone

Shari Henry

I remember that Sunday morning, my class full of wealthy, suburban, trendy-clad sixth-graders. The new girl stood out in her modest clothing. When asked where she went to school, her shy eyes sparkled and an eager smile spread across her face before she said, "My mom teaches me at home."

Expecting the worst from the rest of the class, I tried to change the subject, but to no avail. In unison, the children squealed, "I wish my mom did that!"

That was years ago, long before I ever considered homeschooling. Just today, my eight-year-old son ran outside to play football with another boy home from school on a holiday. The twelve-year-old, a monthly school-fight participant, asked me where TJ went to school. When I said I taught him at home, his quick response echoed my class five years ago, "I wish my mom did that."

I can't count the number of times I've heard the same comment in the years in between, but it's been too many to pretend I don't think homeschooling is best for kids. From now on, when another parent asks me about homeschooling, I'll no longer answer defensively, "Well, it's really not for everybody."

That statement is a lie. Homeschooling may not be best for every parent, but, ideally homeschooling is the best option for every child. There, I said it. Quite frankly, I'm weary of people insinuating that children who'd want to be with their parents all the time, and vice versa, are representative of a sort of unhealthy neediness, or codependency. So-called "child rights" advocates can have their theories, but the truth speaks for itself. And, if we really want to listen to what children are saying, they want to be home. Oh, sure, to varying degrees, some children want to be with other kids more than others, but children want more freedom than any school environment will ever offer, and they want more security, the kind only available at home.

We can't ignore the obvious. Homeschoolers out-perform their conventionally schooled peers academically, psychologically, and despite James J. Kilpatrick's concern about being "cloistered," even socially. Recent research also shows adult homeschoolers grow up to function in and add to our diverse and democratic society. At the risk of being repetitive, in the vast majority of cases, what we have here is not a question of what's best for children, but what parents may or may not want to do or feel capable of doing (perhaps both being equally attributable to being raised in the nation's public schools).

As homeschooling parents, we need to be honest with ourselves and with others. While we shouldn't stand in judgement, by looking squarely at the truth we are better able to help those who may be using us to "test the waters." In most conversations I've had with others, certain themes bubble up time and again. Financial considerations, lack of confidence in one's ability, needy children, and parents worried about losing time to pursue their own interests, are all valid concerns and deserve thoughtful responses.

Obviously, getting along on one income isn't easy. Just as obviously, homeschooling usually requires one parent be home. However, I've seen parents handle financial restraints in creative ways. Some parents work crazy shifts, many work from their homes, and others drastically slash household budgets. As most homeschoolers find out, we've been duped into thinking we need a lot more than we do. I know a good amount of homeschooling families making it on less than $25,000 per year, and some as low as $13,000. I don't want to romanticize this way of life, but it's fair to say that parents and kids feel the lack of material goods is more than offset by the gains of being together.

Aside from financial considerations, many parents really don't believe they're capable of teaching their own kids. "I could never do that" is a commonly heard phrase. Often, I point out the substandard training most teachers receive, spending a good deal of time learning how to control the masses under the guise of "Classroom Management." When it comes to helping kids learn, not only do I think the vast majority of parents are equal to this level of training, I believe they're superior.

What about the really under-educated parents? I once received a phone call from a distraught woman wanting to remove her teenage daughter from school. Her first comment after introducing herself was, "Mrs. Henry, I don't want my daughter to go to school no more and I hear you can help me."

She went on to tell me she didn't know much, but she couldn't stand to watch her child continue to be so sad. Her daughter begged to be homeschooled. It was obvious from this woman's use of the language and things she told me that most people would consider her to be unfit to teach her child much of anything.

I asked her to indulge me while I guessed how her daughter was doing in school. Was she getting a lot of failing grades? Did she have few friends? Her affirmative shriek pierced through the telephone lines.

I suggested that if her daughter was failing school, could barely read, and had no positive social experiences, I didn't see how she, as her mother, could do any worse than the public school. I told her she'd probably love learning side by side with her daughter, and might be surprised at how much she did know, not to mention all the intangibles she had to offer. I gave her some names of other parents with teenagers at home, promised to send her some information, encouraged her to read a few books, and hung up the phone. She called back months later to let me know her daughter was doing fine, reading voraciously, and could learn mostly on her own anyway. Oh, yeah, she was becoming a happy child again. What I didn't say to this mother was I think any public school official who argues that these children, because of a lack of education on their parents' part, are better off with trained professionals (certified teachers), is crazy. First of all, statistics simply wouldn't back them up. Secondly, often children who are in families with less educated parents live in areas where there is less money, and the public schools are even more inferior than those in surrounding wealthier areas. Or, if children live in more monied areas (or are bussed there), they are not treated the same by teachers, and most certainly not by their peers. Public education is not the great equalizer.

What about children with special needs, including children who have been diagnosed with learning disabilities? My personal doubts about these labels aside, these kids may be incredibly tough for parents to deal with, but to think any of them are better off in school is ludicrous. Labeled children are teased by other kids, separated for certain classes, or worse, do their work in "self-contained classrooms," a nice word for cages. Perhaps most devastating of all, these kids often are drugged, legally - ironically, while they're being forced to listen to ridiculous anti-drug propaganda about "just saying no." Many parents have had great success with their "LD" children once they're removed them from school. At home, formerly labeled kids gain self-confidence, learn more readily, get along better with others, and become drug-free. Their learning disabilities virtually disappear.

In less extreme cases, there are children who need a lot of direction, get bored easily, and beg to play with other kids. A mom whom I greatly respect shocked me one day by sharing her frustrations with one of her daughters and whether or not she should be in school. Her husband felt this child's lack of contentment proved she needed to go to school, but the mother, a former teacher, couldn't agree. Since I have a child of similar temperament, I empathized with my friend. These children may need more social outlets than others, especially the kind of spontaneous play provided by a romp in the park or on the neighborhood block. But school doesn't provide these. A 15 minute post-lunch recess and 45 minute gym class simply don't cut it.

More often than not, these kids are highly creative with no appropriate outlets for their creativity during the school day. So, they end up in trouble a lot - I know because I was one of them. I wouldn't sit still, got easily frustrated, and talked back to teachers for entertainment. It's an awful way to spend years of childhood.

Besides, discerning what children need and what they want is one of the toughest parts of being a parent. I often compare socializing to chocolate. We all like both, but too much of either simply isn't good for us. Contrary to the gospel of the status quo, healthy socialization does not equal lots of peer-group socializing. So, while kids may want to play endlessly with other children, it isn't good for them, and we as parents have the tough job of breaking the bad news.

Also, I went on to tell my friend that instead of jampacking my days with activity growing up, I sure wish my parents had forced me to learn to live with boredom. It was the toughest lesson I ever learned, but one which without learning, I may never have found peace of mind or developed creativity.

On the other extreme are the perfect, "gifted" students, though, admittedly, many of these children overlap with the "hyperactive" and highly creative kids. They may thrive in school, but I can't help but think of how wasteful that environment is for them. The best place for extraordinarily bright children to discover their full potential, without the built in ranking and superficial confidence booster of the "gifted" label, is out in the real world with more freedom, more time to pursue their interests, and more opportunity to see others who are highly gifted in different areas which may never have been recognized in school.

Among the most unexpected remarks I've heard from parents who say they couldn't homeschool are "I couldn't stand to be with my kids all day! They'd drive me crazy! What do you do? How do you find time for yourself?" To these forthright questions, I can only return honest answers. Sometimes my kids do drive me crazy. Sometimes I wonder if I'll ever get to finish a shower or use the toilet without being interrupted with a burning question, a fight that needs resolution, or a "Mom, come look!" But, all in all, most homeschooling families, ours included, seem to settle into a nice daily rhythm. I like it when Earl Stevens says homeschooling is about learning to live sanely. Without pressures to get out the door, catch a bus, be picked up on time (always when the baby goes down for a nap), days flow more smoothly. Leisurely walks open up the world to me in a new way, looking for animal tracks, racing across a field, or stopping to take in the blood red southern sky. Most days, my kids have had their fill of me by noon or so, and are perfectly content to play quietly so I can read, nap with the baby, or write. They take my writing seriously because they live with it and because I take their interests seriously.

It's easier to raise little ones with the older ones around to help. I'm dead serious when I tell people I don't know what I'd do if TJ was in school all day, since, like most homeschooled kids, he's very capable despite his youth. Life with three kids is much easier than life was with just one, in large part due to having the older ones around to help. This kind of concrete participation in the world around them contributes immeasurably to children's sense of self-worth in a way straight "A's", winning the 60-yard dash, or a paper laden with smiley faces never could.

For now, it's not enough for me to be a parents' rights, school choice, or free-market education advocate. When push comes to shove, after years of listening to children, I can't help but remain a purist to the homeschooling cause. Admittedly, this is not a politically astute or even practical position. But matters of the heart seldom are.

From the January-February, 1994 issue of *Home Education Magazine*.

Part Two

TEACHING and LEARNING

What It Takes to be a Good Home Teacher

Mario Pagnoni

People often say to me, "Well, sure, you're qualified to home school — you're a teacher — but I could never do it." Too many parents feel this way. They think they're unable to teach because they're not clever enough, or well trained enough, or disciplined, either.

According to one college professor, "The education majors aren't very bright, but they're nice, decent, polite kids. I like them very much." It pains me to say this — but I agree. The majority of teachers I've encountered are well meaning but somewhat out of touch with young people and their concerns. They are preoccupied with maintaining discipline and teaching facts and they are buried under a mountain of paperwork and other non-teaching duties. As a work force, they are easily regimented and too timid to make waves. If you think they can do something for your children that you cannot, you just may be selling yourself short.

I think I'm a good home teacher. I have qualities that make me good at it. Some people, because they have no teaching credentials, have trouble convincing people that they are competent to teach their children. I have trouble convincing people that the reasons I'm competent to teach my own children have little or nothing to do with my teaching credentials or college background.

I'm good at home teaching because I love my children and enjoy their company. Helping them find answers to their questions and sharing in their exploration of the world is my joy. I like their company. I'd much rather play ball together in our neighborhood than shuffle them off to Little League.

I'm good at it because I consider my boys two of my closest friends. Like my other friends, they're people I want to be around — for work or play. We can talk openly and honestly on any subject. We can rely on each other.

I'm also good at it because I can identify with children. This is a prime parenting skill. It is essential to be able to relate to children — to recall how is was to be very young, how different your concerns were, how much more fragile your dignity was. You have to be able to focus on their needs, only one of which is the need to learn.

Finally, I'm a good home educator because I have a sense of humor (essential), am literate (helpful), like learning, don't take it *too* seriously, am patient, trust my children, and have confidence in them and in myself. Certainly you possess many of these traits and a great deal more that I don't. These are nothing more than good parenting skills and good parenting skills are good home teaching skills. You *can* home school, and be good at it. Many people are doing that already, in every state in the U.S.A. They are having good academic results, and, as an added dividend, are finding their lives enriched because of the experience.

Confidence is an important quality for home schoolers (both teachers and students). In my experience with children I don't see many with self confidence. Not enough adults have it, either.

What we do see in schools are a lot of insecure young people with negative self concepts. That's partly because kids don't get much praise. We don't tell them how good they are. We should. It would help. We don't give them enough tasks to do, so that they can develop responsibility and a sense of accomplishment. Moreover, parents and children don't do enough things together so as to share in the building of these good feelings. I'd like to share a story about confidence.

During the summers of my college years, I played baseball in a league that featured the area's top college players. My teammate one summer was a fellow who didn't have a great deal of talent but who had nevertheless distinguished himself as a ballplayer. His play was fundamentally sound. His skills were only adequate. But he was a fierce competitor who always helped the team. Describing him, opponents would say, "He can't do much — just beat you."

At season's end he was voted the most outstanding college player in the league. Over the course of the season we had become good friends but, though he played well and deserved the award, I was jealous. What bothered me was that (like some others in the league) I could outhit, outrun, and outthrow him. He knew it, too. "I wish I had your talent," he'd say. "I wish I had your award," was my retort.

I could never fathom what made him excell despite his lack of first-rate skills. During one ball game I found out. He was batting second in the line-up and I third. Our team had the winning run on base in the last inning of an important game. My friend and I talked in the on-deck circle. I remember thinking to myself, "God, I hope someone gets a hit to win this game before I get up." His attitude was so different. "Looks like I'm going to get a chance to win this one," he said excitedly. He wanted to bat. I didn't. I had all I could do to settle the butterflies in my stomach. A minute later he drilled a game-ending base hit. Elated, I helped carry him off the field. Watching this episode unfold made things clear to me. *That's* why he's an outstanding college player. He believes in himself and gets the most out of every ounce of talent he has. That's what we've got to do — and that's what we've got to help our children do.

I haven't seen or heard from my "talentless" friend for ten years, but even if I did I couldn't thank him enough for the lesson he taught me. It came a little late for my ballplaying career, but not too late for my life. I know realistically what I can and cannot do. I'm even a little cocky nowadays. People don't like that. They prefer the phony "aw shucks... I'm not so good" attitude. But I am good at lots of things — not great, but good. The first step you can take toward good home education is to believe in yourself. You *can* be a competent home teacher. Portraying that confidence in your home teaching is the first step in building confident students.

From the May, 1986 issue of *Home Education Magazine*.

Basic Skills versus Knowledge

Kathleen McCurdy

Basic skills are acquired abilities. We are not born with them, we have to learn them. Furthermore, skills can be lost through disuse. They require drill or practice. Does this make you think of flash cards or multiplication tables? Instead, consider walking. Walking is a very basic skill. It would be hard to make it in this world if we all lost our ability to walk (though science fiction writers may predict otherwise).

Most of us acquire the ability to walk near the time of our first birthday. Though not very skillful at it yet, we somehow figured out the process and began taking steps, usually with a very definite goal in mind (that vase on the table or the open front door). But did you ever see a parent urging his child to *practice* walking? Some of us may have panicked when Timmy passed his first birthday without taking that first step. We may have coaxed and prodded, and maybe even bribed with a cookie or toy, to get him to let go and start walking. But once those first toddling steps are ventured, we usually give no further thought to the difficult process of mastering the skill of walking.

And yet, every normal child proceeds to practice and drill, day after day, without the slightest prompting on our part, until at last the skill is mastered and he can walk without thinking about it. One of our five was born with an extra measure of ambition. He would walk before the others had. At eight months he would walk, he would! He found out that falling was involved, so he practiced falling. At seven months he mastered the art of falling without hurting so as to get on with the process of walking. We laughed, watching him. We surely never asked him to practice falling! But at eight and a half months he walked across the living room. At ten months he was walking out the door!

So what about the flash cards and multiplication tables? Where do they come in? Well, not yet. First we have to settle on what are the basic skills. Walking is, and so is talking. They all learn to talk without thinking about it (sad to say). What about eating with a fork, or tying your shoelaces? Don't most kids learn to ride a bike if they have a chance? And who is asking who about taking the car out for a practice run? Yes, driving is a basic skill in our society.

Well, what about reading? Do you have to urge your child to practice reading? Reading is certainly a basic skill. Why don't they learn it like the other skills we mentioned? They do — if we're patient. First, we have to wait until the child is ready to learn. How many of us have tried to potty train a child at fifteen months — with dismal results — only to find he trained himself at thirty months when he was ready? Second, if it's a basic skill, we must be good at it ourselves. Our example is important. Do we read? Does the child see us read? Do we read to him?

The reason a child masters walking is not so he can say he walks. It's so he can get to where he's going. He wants to investigate things, find out where the path leads. Once he becomes aware that books and magazines can inform and entertain, he won't stop until he has mastered the skill of reading also. So third, the child must see its usefulness.

Here is where the flash cards and multiplication tables come in. Did you hate them? Maybe they really weren't relevant. There may be more than one way to learn a skill. Some kids learn to ride a bike by practicing with training wheels. Others start right out with a full sized bike. I recently asked my son, the one who's a whiz at math, if he'd ever learned his multiplication tables. This young electronics engineer said he'd learned them three different times as a kid. "But I still can't tell you what seven times eight is," he said. "I know the ones I use the most, and I figure out the others as I go."

So maybe some things are more "basic" than others. Let's say that the ability to multiply is a basic skill, but maybe the tables are not. And this leads us to the fourth point, which is that some skills are more basic than others depending on your natural talents and aptitudes. For instance, being able to carry a tune is a basic skill for a musician, but not necessarily for a writer or a painter. A child with an artistic bent may spend hours sharpening his drawing skills, even without encouragement, but have little time to practice his spelling.

Now what about knowledge. Knowledge is not something that you can practice. This was discovered in the dark ages when students were required to recite all the kings of European dynasties, together with the dates of their reigns and the names of their wives and concubines. They were also expected to conjugate Latin verbs and parrot other more or less useless stuff. Yet how many chemistry students have labored to memorize the periodic table of elements and their atomic weights, etc., only to forget such information as soon as the mid-term test was over? Very simply, such knowledge is not retained.

Knowledge is an organized collection of meaningful facts. But the organizing is in the mind, not in someone's textbook. Children will pick up knowledge wherever it may be found, as long as it is meaningful to them. Which means as long as they can relate it to what they already know. (Or if they think it's something you didn't especially want them to learn.)For instance, before the hostage crisis how many of us were informed about the geographic location of Iran? Hang a map of the world on the kitchen wall and listen to the news every morning. Your kids will learn more geography than you'd ever dream possible. Or dig up some stories about your great, great uncle who fought in the Civil War, and see how interested they become in the issues that separated the North from the South. Soon the whole history of America may attract their attention. Or order up a volcanic eruption and then leave around some books on geology and maybe even meteorology. Lots of learning will take place spontaneously.

Available information plus a reason to know is all it takes to provide children with an extensive fund of knowledge. So who needs school? Those who think that children's minds are just like empty bottles waiting to be filled. But the mind is like a sponge, absorbing whatever is available. Rather, it is more like a hunter out looking for sustenance or pleasure.

What do we do then, if we want our child to master a certain basic skill? First, determine if he's ready. Maturity, previous experience and accessory skills are involved here. Second, provide an example to model after. Parental example is most important here. Third, find a motivating factor. It has to be useful, interesting, important or marketable. Fourth, make sure the child has enough aptitude to make it worthwhile. Just like some kids aren't built for contact sports, others were just never meant to comprehend algebra.

And how can we ensure that our child acquires sufficient knowledge? First, answer his questions. When a child is asking questions, he's learning. Second, make information relevant. For instance, if Grandma just had cataract surgery, a knowledge of optics may suddenly become relevant. Third, provide enough reference tools. Maps, dictionaries, encyclopedias, etc., should be handy when you need them. Even a good high school or college textbook can be used as a reference for answering pertinent questions or looking up facts. Think of it as building a wall of knowledge, with each fact a brick, and the mortar of experience holding it all together.

This kind of education is invaluable, and won't be discarded as soon as summer arrives. It is the stuff that great men are made of — self-made men, who know, and know that they know.

From the August, 1986 issue of *Home Education Magazine.*

Answers to a Mother's Questions

John Holt

Question: My greatest concern is that I don't want to slant my children's view of life all through "mother colored" glasses...

Answer: If you mean determine your children's view of life, you couldn't do it even if you wanted to. You are an influence on your children, and an important one, but by no means the only one, or even the only important one. How they later see the world is going to be determined by a great many things, many of them probably not to your liking, and most of them out of your control. On the other hand, it would be impossible, even if you wanted to, not to have *some* influence on your children's view of life.

Question: I also wonder if I can have the thoroughness, the follow through demanded, the patience, and the continuing enthusiasm for a diversity of interests they will undoubtedly have.

Answer: Well, who in any school would have more, or even as much? I was a good student in the "best" schools, and very few adults there were even slightly concerned with my interests. Beyond that, you may expect too much of yourself. Your children's learning is not all going to come from you, but from *them*, and their interaction with the world around them, which of course includes you. You do not have to know everything they want to know, or be interested in everything they are interested in. As for patience, maybe you won't have enough at first; like many home teaching parents, you may start by trying to do too much. But like the rest, you will learn from experience - mostly, to trust your children.

Question: I get the impression that most unschoolers live on farms growing their own vegetables (which I'd like) or have unique lifestyles in urban areas, and heavy father participation in children's education. What about suburbanites with modern convenienced homes and fathers who work for a company 10 to 12 hours a day away from home? What difference will this make? Will unschooling work as well?

Answer: Well enough. You and your children will have to find out as you go along what differences they make, and deal with them as best you can. Once, people said that the suburbs were the best of all possible worlds in which to bring up children; now it is the fashion to say they are the worst. Both views are exaggerated. In city, country, or suburb, there is more than enough to give young people an interesting world to grow up in, plenty of food for thought and action. You don't have to have everything in the way of resources for your children, and if you did, they wouldn't have enough time to make use of all of it.

Question: Isn't the father's involvement crucial?

Answer: It can certainly be helpful, but it is not crucial. Some of the most successful unschoolers we know of are single mothers. And there may be many others that we don't know about.

Question: What if the children want to go to school?

Answer: This is a hard question. There is more than one answer to it, and these often conflict. Parents could argue, as some do, that since they believe that school can and probably will do their children deep and lasting harm, they have as much right to keep them out, even if they want to go, as they would to tell them not to play on a pile of radioactive wastes. This argument seems more weighty in the case of younger children, who could not be expected to understand how school might hurt them. If somewhat older children said determindedly and often, and for good reasons, that they really wanted to go to school, I would tend to say, let them go. How much older? What are good reasons? I don't know. A bad reason might be, "The other kids tell me that at school lunch you can have chocolate milk."

Question: Since people feel that as a religious group (Christian Scientists) we neglect our children (which is not the case), I'm concerned that someone might be eager to take us to court and take away our children.

Answer: The schools in a number of cases have tried - shamefully - to take children away from unschooling parents. I think there are legal counters to this, strategies that would make it highly unlikely that a court would take such action. And if worse came to worst, and a court said, "Put your children back in school or we'll take them away," you can always put them back in while you plan what to do next — which might be simply to move to another state or even school or judicial district.

Question: I don't want to feel I'm sheltering my children or running away from adversity.

Answer: Why not? It is your right, and your proper business, as parents, to shelter your children and protect them from adversity, at least as much as you can. Many of the world's children are starved or malnourished, but you would not starve your children so that they would know what this was like. You would not let your children play in the middle of a street full of high speed traffic. Your business is, as far as you can, to help them realize their human potential, and to that end you put as much as you can of good into their lives, and keep out as much as you can of bad. If you think - as you do - that school is bad, then it is clear what you should do.

Question: I value their learning how to handle challenges or problems...

Answer: There will be plenty of these. Growing up was probably never easy, and it is particularly hard in a world as anxious, confused, and fear-ridden as ours. To learn to know oneself, and to find a life worth living and work worth doing, is problem and challenge enough, without having to waste time on the fake and unworthy challenges of school - pleasing the teacher, staying out of trouble, fitting in with the gang, being popular, doing what everyone else does.

Question: Will they have the opportunity to overcome or do things that they think they don't want to do?

Answer: I'm not sure what this question means. If it means, will unschooled children know what it is to have to do difficult and demanding things in order to reach goals they have set for themselves, I would say, yes, life is full of such requirements. But this is not at all the same thing as doing something, and in the case of schools usually something boring and stupid, simply because someone else tells you you'll be punished if you don't. Whether children resist such demands or yield to them, it is bad for them. Struggling with the inherent difficulties of a chosen or inescapable task builds character; merely submitting to a superior force destroys it.

From the May, 1985 issue of *Home Education Magazine.*

Unit Study Approach

Lee Gonet

I truly believe in and practice the unit study approach to learning, using available resources other than standardized textbooks. A recent example of this learning style is the dinosaur unit my 3 and 6 year olds studied this past summer (yes, we have school all year round!).

My children first showed an interest in dinosaurs while playing with a friend. For days afterwards I heard lots of "fantasy play" concerning these giant creatures. Off to the library we went and every week for the next six weeks we checked out dinosaur books. These are some of our favorites: *Dinosaurs-A Lost World*, by Keith Moseley; *A Dozen Dinosaurs*, by Richard Armour; *Dinosaurs and Other Prehistoric Animals*, by Darlene Geis; and *Whatever Happened to Patrick's Dinosaur?*, by Carol Carrick.

Jessi, our six-year-old, even made her own dinosaur book! She drew 13 different pictures, labeling each one by copying the names out of her books (she doesn't read yet). Jessi even made cover pages, bound the book with string and included a table of contents with the meaning of the name of each dinosaur. We now use her book as a reference in our science section (this type of activity is an excellent record for showing to people who are skeptical about your home schooling, such as relatives, friends, and nosy neighbors).

We also checked out an album called *Dinosaur Rock*, by Valeri and Stein. The children's favorite song was one called "The Little Bitty Babies and the Great Big Momma..." so, back to the library to find a book on dinosaur eggs and "child care": *Dinosaurs and Their Young*, by Russell Freedman. Then a friend introduced us to a story album

(also available at the library) called *Little Blue*, about a young bron-
tosaurus. The children listened to this album for hours.

The final book we checked out described how to build paper mache
sculptures of dinosaurs. So out came the flour paste, newspapers, sty-
rofoam, paint, and 3 excited children-we invited the friend that started it all to join us. It took about a week to build our sculptures, but
we all had a good time, and the library put the finished models on display for a couple of months!

The children were all very proud of a job well done, and even
Patrick, our 3-year-old, can tell the difference between a brachiosaurus
and a diplodocus! This mom was happy too, because we had discovered every "school" subject possible without the textbook grind: science, writing, music, phonics, practical skills, math, history, geography, drama, art, spiritual studies (I taught the creationist view), reading, even "social time".

Our unit study project now is "weather reporting," with Jessi filling
out a chart on the daily sky conditions. She is learning to tell time,
read a thermometer, identify clouds, and wind direction. We have
worked on odd and even numbers, counting by two's (marks on a
thermometer), water evaporation, made a wind vane, and even plan to
make a home made barometer! Again, we are learning much more
than just meteorology!

As a parent, I encourage every family to try unit studies as an exciting and motivating way to learn!

From the April, 1987 issue of *Home Education Magazine*.

Sharing Enthusiasm for Learning

Kathleen McCurdy

Many parents, being themselves a product of mass education, have little taste for learning. They have struggled through the learning process to the bitter end, always anticipating the glorious finale when they could throw away the books and get on with the business of living. The only thing that made life tolerable was the social aspect of school — fleeting moments of communicating with their friends on the playground or between classes, studying the idiosyncrasies of the teachers, or computing the preponderance of certain behavior fashions or verbal expressions to determine a consensus among their peers. (Could this be why the "social aspect" is such a burning question among critics of home schooling?)

But disassociated from school, learning can be very exciting. For instance, many of us have hobbies or avocations that we have picked up simply through a process of satisfying our curiosity. Whether it is learning the advertised virtues of late model cars because we are preparing to go down and buy one, or perfecting the skill of cake decorating, or learning a new recipe for zucchini bread, we are likely to continue learning throughout our adult lives.

Try this: sit down and make a list of the subjects you are the most fascinated by, the ones you spend time reading about or pursuing in other ways. It might be the use of herbs and natural healing, collecting low calorie gourmet recipes, studying the psychology of soap operas, or the history (gossip?) of your neighborhood, the philosophy underlying the Constitution of the United States, the care and training of horses, restoring old cars, how to invest your fortune, or traditions about large hairy apes inhabiting the northwest, etc., etc. (well, what *do* you do in your spare time?)

Now think about how you might share these interests with your children. If you are poking herbs down them, chances are they will be curious about how it will help. If they know what type of recipes you are looking for, they might start cutting them out of the paper for you. As a child of nine or ten I discovered that my dad enjoyed *Reader's Digest*-type jokes. For his birthday I mutilated some old copies of the magazine and created a scrapbook for his amusement. In the process I discovered that the *Digest* was a pretty interesting magazine, and began reading it avidly myself — and so, no doubt, improved my reading skills.

Children tend to be great imitators, and parents are their first role models. If something interests you, chances are it will also become of interest to them. The important thing here is that you are not teaching them skills that they must learn "for their own good" and for which they can see no good use at the moment. Instead you are sharing something with them that means a lot to you. It is a "grown-up" activity and provides an opportunity for them to share in your enthusiasm for learning. In the process they are picking up skills that are essential, but they'll hardly be aware of it because they are having fun.

My mother loves music and I remember sitting under the piano listening to her practice. She began reading stories of great composers to me. One of her books had short biographical notes and this lead to discussions, longer biographies, and in turn developed into an interest in the history of music. Though she never had time to become proficient in piano, the effort she made to share her enthusiasm with me paid off, for I later became a pianist and music teacher.

Another benefit inherent in this sharing process is that children learn how to learn, in the sense that if they have questions about something that interests them, they will be able to recall how their parents went about doing their own research. They will know that the answers are out there and they will have a good idea of how to go about finding them, just like mom and dad. This can give a child's self confidence a real boost.

From the June, 1986 issue of *Home Education Magazine*.

Expert Advice

Steve Thom

expert/ eks 'poit/(L. expoitus fr.ex used to be + poitus on the ball)

When I decided to home school it was like learning to sky dive. Intellectually, we knew that lots were doing it successfully. Emotionally, we expected to be the one freak accident. "Well, Tom, we just don't know what happened. Their chute just kinda disappeared."

All of our lives we've depended on the "expert" to show us the way; to do our thinking for us; to sift through the information explosion. And here we are throwing the rascals out. As home schoolers, we're saying to the education professionals, "Thanks, but no thanks, so long, auf Weidersehen to yooooou." These are the same people and theories that we, and our parents, have depended upon all of our lives. The very same ones who taught us, and we turned out alright, didn't we? Pretty radical stuff, this.

At first this felt great. We were boldly going where no man had gone before. Climbing the high dive platform is exhilarating; being there is a different story. Naturally, the first thing we did to fill this "expert" void was to seek out new "experts."

Well, home schooling didn't disappoint us. There were more than enough "professionals" to go around. And like all good experts, they offer conflicting advice:

"Parents don't need any special educational background; parents should consider returning to college."

"Home schooling is easy; home schooling is difficult."

"Co-operate with the authorities; fight them tooth and nail."

"Go ahead and use packaged curriculums; only intellectual wimps use packaged curriculums."

"Use workbooks and drill; never use workbooks."

"All courses should be Christian based; Bible should be studied separately."

"Spend lots of time with other home schoolers; be independent."

"Test; don't test."

"Study every day; five days a week; four days a week."

"Never watch television; use television as an educational tool."

"Children need lots of socialization; the extended family provides all the socialization necessary."

One of the great advantages of home schooling is that we can maximize our feelings of self-doubt: as human beings, adults, parents, and now as teachers. We read about home educators who have been at it for ten years; with eleven children; hiding in the attic from truant officers; going to jail. All we have is three children and nobody harassing us. And still we are having problems. We must really be lame. What's wrong with us?

What's wrong with us is that we're suffering from information overload. It's similar to a criminal trial in which one psychiatric "expert" says, "This guy is totally bonkers," and another one says, "This guy is totally sane." A little learning may be a dangerous thing, but a lot of learning will scramble your medulla oblongata.

When we have days of doubt regarding home schooling, we can count on the educational establishment to set us right back on track. A friend of ours is going to college to become an elementary school teacher. Her first required course has the lofty title: Fundamentals of Education. The first test had questions like: "Which state in the union has the lowest wage scale for teachers?" Thank you, I needed that.

When we have days of doubt regarding the best way to home school we no longer consult John Holt, the Moores, or our twelve foot stack of magazines, manuals, catalogs, and case histories. If something isn't working we drop it, pure and simple. The only "experts" we feel a need to consult are the members of our household. The good Lord has given us intuition and common sense; we've decided to use it.

Now that we're "experts", we've come to some pretty radical conclusions. If you love your children, you are the best teacher they can possibly have. And you don't need to take Fundamentals of Education to do it. You know them: their strengths and weaknesses, their needs. You won't turn them into emotional wrecks through cruel and stifling criticism. You won't force them to conform to some bizarre set of standards. You won't sedate their minds with pointless and idiotic repetition or with material that's too difficult. You won't stifle their curiosity or creativity.

The subject is not really teaching, it's learning. Teaching is like stuffing little link sausages til they burst. That's public education. In learning, our task is to clear the path and then get out of the way. That's home education.

Now, I'm not advocating throwing out the proverbial baby with the bath water. We are very much indebted to those who came before us.

Without them, we never would have embarked on this great adventure. But when "they" disagree, we are faced with the task of making our own decisions, being the captains of our own fate. (Can I turn a cliche, or what?) Once you get used to it, it's quite enlightening. You begin to question all sorts of "expert" advice. Home schooling is good for parents and other living things.

This new attitude grants the gift of intellectual freedom. Now people ask, "Why do you home school?" I still answer with the standard litany of whimpering excuses. I hate to offend anyone. But now I realize that the question should really be, "Why would anyone consider sending their children to public school?" No longer do I feel the nagging guilt and doubts associated with home schooling. It's possible to read home education materials without constantly saying,"We should be doing that, we ought to be doing that, why can't we do that?" If it sounds good we try it. If it suits us, great; if it doesn't, fine. And so it goes.

So what is my expert advice? I don't have any unless you're going to live with us. Pick and choose. Do what works for you, discard what doesn't. And above all don't feel guilty or apologize. And permit other home schoolers to do the same.

And remember what I always say, "It'll get better."

From the April, 1987 issue of *Home Education Magazine*.

Is That All He Ever Talks About?

Pat Mitchell-Erwin

"Is that all he ever talks about?"

My four year old son Ryan's fascination with dinosaurs, dragons, and creatures with similar features drew this question from my father on a recent visit. Amidst concern from a doubting family that he was being limited by what seemed a narrow range of interests, my first reaction as a homeschooling parent was to become defensive and worried at the same time. "What if they're right? Could it be that I've overlooked something in my child's experiences?" Fortunately my next reaction was that of a student of child development. That was to evaluate exactly what this apparent single-mindedness had contributed to my son's development.

The most salient developmental strides have been in the area of language acquisition and use. Indeed, language is the area of development most rapid and visible during the period from about two to five years, and Ryan competently uses both everyday and scientific vocabulary. Words such as Tryannosaurus Rex, Ankylosaurus, fossil, omniverous, and extinct make their way correctly into his sentences. Statements such as "Dimetrodon means two sizes of teeth" and "Pterodactyl means winged-finger" are meant to impress us daily. This rote memorization of words and meanings seems useless in terms of teaching theory at this stage and it is likely he won't even remember those facts when he is older. That isn't important. What is important is the evolving ability to relate word roots to specific meanings which will be stored away and used as he achieves more mature vocabulary capabilities.

I have observed a tremendous increase in Ryan's overall language use as a result of playing with dinosaur figures. His imagination is stimulated by books we read and films he sees and he makes his own dramas using the plastic models. He is able to substitute the names of dinosaurs for other animals in songs and stories, complete with changing the attributes and motions to fit.

Much of the preschooler's language is egocentric; that is, speech where no two-way communication is taking place. The dinosaur figures provide the vehicle for practice of symbolic thinking as well as the basis of a dramatic monologue. The beginnings of inter-communicative skills are enhanced by use of the dinosaurs to carry on a "conversation."

Dramatic play and development of motor skills have been influenced together by dinosaurs. With a belt or rope attached to the back of his pants, Ryan is instantly transformed into Tyrannosaurus rex, Stegosaurus or Anatosaurus. After months of using the same stance and walk for all types, he began to observe differences in books and television programs and adjusted his dramatic play accordingly.

Ryan's love of dinosaurs has impacted his social development as well. He's always been a high-need child who was very slow to warm up to people outside his immediate family. I have seen dinosaur play become a common focus for social interaction with children he had never before met. The children "talk shop", so to speak, comparing dinosaurs and creating dialogue. His knowledge of dinosaur names and characteristics has also given him something he is confident of, and is proud to share with adults. He now makes acquaintances easily at the park and beach and has become a delightful conversationalist with any adult who will take the time to listen.

Power is another aspect of dinosaur play which has influenced social development. Being one of the youngest in the family (number four of five boys), he is often left powerless by his older brothers. However, Tyrannosaurus rex can do anything, beat anyone, and masters everything. It also helps him deal with the frustrations associated with having a baby brother. He knows that it is unacceptable to physically harm the baby, yet, through Tyrannosaurus rex he can exert some control even if it is over a less powerful dinosaur.

Children of this age are quite interested in classifying everything around them in order to make sense of their worlds. Dinosaurs have provided the perfect vehicle with which to develop this and other math and science skills. They can be classified by size, diet, habitat, morphological features such as horns, wings, scales, claws, et cetera. They are counted, sorted, observed, and categorized. In the process, the dinosaurs are inevitably compared with the features of living animals he knows about. It is not unusual to hear Ryan repeat the features of a reptile or mammal aloud to compare a prehistoric creature to a living one.

Progression of observation skills has been exemplified by Ryan's ability to discriminate among the three dinosaurs which superficially look very much alike. Among Styracosaurus, Monoclonius and Triceratops the main difference is the head morphology. He can now

instantly recognize any of the three and include the appropriate features in his clay figures.

Dinosaurs have provided just the stimulation my son needed to
pursue artistic activities. He had not been interested in coloring or
drawing until age four when he spontaneously began to draw -
dinosaurs, of course! These first drawings were primitive, similar to
those of a two and a half or three year old's. The drawings rapidly
increased in maturity and in detail. Similar interest in working with
clay and sand has been generated by the interest in dinosaurs.
Evidence of increasing observation and dexterity can be seen in his
clay figures. In just a few months they have progressed from "blobs"
called dinosaurs to figures in which small details such as the correct
number of horns, different tails, wings, or types of mouths are included.

It became evident through this evaluation that much more was
going on than simply a single-minded fascination with large, non-
existent creatures. All of these developmental areas have been fostered
in a natural, stress-free way with my role being only that of facilitator.
It was not necessary to contrive "teaching sessions" for my child to
learn numbers, shapes, language skills, colors, social skills, observation
techniques and many other skills. All that was necessary was for me to
be involved enough to notice his interests and provide some appropriate books, toys, and materials. His natural desire to learn about and
organize his world has done the rest. And even though doubt prompted me to evaluate the quality of my child's preschool experience, I
have emerged more convinced than ever that I am - and will remain -
his best teacher!

From the August, 1987 issue of *Home Education Magazine.*

The Most Meaningful Lesson

Chris Ressler

On a bright sunny day last fall, my good friend Jean called up and asked if I and my three children would like to join her and her group of four on a pumpkin harvest. They were on their way to a local U-Pick farm to select their would-be Jack-O'-Lanterns, and it sounded like a wonderful adventure. Coats were gathered, a quick snack was fixed for the trip, and soon Jean's familiar impatient *honk* sounded in the driveway. We were off, laughing and giggling all the way.

It was about twenty miles to the U-Pick farm, but everyone was in such high spirits that we were there in no time at all. Out piled the kids, wondering loudly at the sights and sounds of a real working farm. Two big geese came scuttling over and greeted us, a beautiful big collie chased them away and assumed the duties that were rightfully his. Brown-eyed cows watched us, and chickens scattered from under the feet of the approaching farmer.

Soon each child had chosen the "perfect" pumpkin for carving, and we loaded nine of them into the car. Jean and I were paying for the prizes when the farmer nodded toward the children, racing up and down the lane with his collie. "Does my heart good to see a bunch of youngsters get out of school for a trip out into the country!"

Jean and I looked at each other for a brief moment, and then she smiled. "These kids aren't out of school... they're in it right now!" And between us, we attempted to explain how we taught our kids at home. We needn't have tried so hard to convince this kind gentleman... he thought it was a marvelous idea! For the next half hour he told us about how his own father has gotten fed up with the school he'd attended and quit at age 14, working until he'd saved enough for a down payment on this very farm. And he himself had dropped out of school in the eighth grade to assume the responsibilities of the farm when his father passed away. At the time it had been a matter of necessity, but he had long since decided that it was probably one of the best things that had ever happened to him.

"Why don't you come on back one of these days and we'll show those youngsters more about the farm?" he suggested. We agreed, and a wonderful friendship has since grown. Our families have spent many delightful afternoons helping out with farm chores, and we've spent the weekend several times now, camping in a stately grove of trees whose beauty rivals that of many well-tended parks. And our new-found friend? He seems to beam with pleasure each time our cars pull into the driveway of his farm. He once confided that his own family doesn't visit him and his wife as much as they'd like, and in a way, we've been "adopted" by these wise and wonderful folks. They've come to our home in town three or four times now, and always delight in taking two or three of the children to a museum, a fair, or a special show. Having such remarkable people as friends has enriched all our lives. My son Seth, now 15, has announced that he'd like to be a farmer when he grows up... quite a switch from his prior ambition - a rock star!

Homeschooling has changed our lives in so many ways. When our family travels now we often spend a lot of time beforehand searching out historic places or interesting sites to visit. Our birthday and Christmas gifts are more apt to be educational in nature - though no less appreciated. For Seth's birthday we gave him a real microscope; 12 year old daughter Julie received a much-longed-for electric typewriter of her own for Christmas last year. As parents, both my husband and I have found ourselves taking much more time to answer questions, to explain things, to listen, and to appreciate the wonderful relationship we have with our youngsters.

Four years ago, when our children were still in school, it seemed as though our entire lives were run by the schedule the kids brought home at the beginning of the school year. I found myself looking forward to weekends as much as they did, and wondering vaguely why. Like most parents, my husband and I just assumed that school was the best place for our kids, but when a friend mentioned an article about homeschooling one day it seemed as though I'd found the answer to a question I didn't even know I'd asked! My husband, always an open-minded sort, was mostly curious about why we hadn't looked into the idea before. It was as though we had assumed that going to school was simply something children *did* - no questions asked, and when we finally learned to ask those questions, we felt somehow cheated by the years our children had been away from us.

Our local homeschooling newsletter asked the following question in a recent issue: "What is the most meaningful thing you have learned as a result of your family's home schooling?" I answered the question this way: "When I first read this month's question I didn't think that I could narrow all the wonderful things we've learned down to just one. The sharing, the caring, the friendships, the special times, learning to trust myself and my children's abilities... there's been so much! But after a while I realized that there is one lesson that stands out in my mind. I've learned that time is precious, irretrievable, and that we should make every effort to make these years with our families all that they can be. When my oldest son, now 15, was born, I thought he'd be a baby forever. But last week he drove me down to the store! As I sat there beside him, trying hard not to be conspicuous, I realized that he was taking charge of his own life now, and that within a year or two he'd be off into the world on his own, making his own decisions, as he should. But he was with us for such a short while! Who could have dreamed that time would fly by so quickly?

"Memory pictures my little four year old splashing in her wading pool; then yesterday my almost-grown young lady fixed fried chicken - and it was as good as any I've ever made.

Our children grow up so quickly, we have so little time with them. It ticks silently away even as we sit here and watch it. And then one day, without realizing that it's even gone, we wonder where it all went. As homeschooling families, we are actually blessed. Our children are at home with us, instead of spending the better part of their young lives trying to please nameless teachers and administrators. We can build so many more precious memories. We need only be willing to take the time."

I've taped that to my mirror, and I read it whenever I need to remind myself to be more patient, more understanding, less of a perfectionist, or less involved in things that really don't matter. It hasn't been easy, but I'm learning to watch for those all important chances to do things with my children. Not for them... with them. I read the other day that one of the greatest delights of any child's life is when his or her mother or father takes the time to do something with them - to play a game, read a book, draw pictures, or go for a walk with just that child. The author was referring to preschool-age children, but it's true for children of any age. Our time is one of the most valuable - and valued - gifts we can give. Who better to give it to than our children?

From the January-February, 1988 issue of *Home Education Magazine*.

Part Three

SUBJECTS ONE TWO THREE

READING/WRITING

Part Three - Subjects One Two Three

Benefits of Later Literacy

Penny Barker

In the late 1960's, when I had my first baby, the talk among mothers was of toilet training - how early to train, how late to train, or whether to just wait for our toddlers to do it themselves. By the time I had my fifth baby in the late '70's, the topic of conversation had changed to nursing and the age a baby should be weaned - how early, how late, or whether to just let the baby do the weaning himself. Now in the '80's I find parents (not just mothers now) anxious to hear about the age at which their child begins to read. The current reading question among parents of children who are either home schooled or into some form of alternative education seems to be the same - early, late, or just let it happen?

In my own work with my five homeschooled children as well as the scores of other children I've known and worked with over the past 16 years, I have come to see some benefits for those who come to the process of reading later. By later, I mean at an age past the generally accepted one of six, which as been set by the traditional school system.

I think it is important for parents to have a clear understanding of just what reading is, since we sometimes confuse one's ability to read with one's intelligence. Reading is the footpath to secondary information, in contrast to primary information, which is what we take into our brain through our own experience or through interaction with the source of information. In my experience with children I have found that it is not what he takes in second-hand that a child really knows, so much as what he, himself, actually experiences that becomes the foundation of his intelligence. Primary information comes first, secondary afterwards, and together these form the basis of knowledge. In fact, throughout one's life the proportion of primary to secondary information has much to do with the quality of one's life. I'm sure you can all relate to that feeling of having done too much "head" work and feeling the need to get outside to take a walk or work in the garden. I've noticed over the years I've worked with children that they seem most balanced when they spend a good deal of time "doing." The experiences they gain from their physical involvement with the environment seem to give them something tangible on which to form their ideas about the world.

I remember when Britt was 15 and she and Maggie (aged 10) and Dan (aged 9) would go off on birding hikes. Only Britt was a reader, so when the others spotted a bird and found a photo of it in the field guide, they would take the guide to Britt so she could help with the identification details. Maggie and Dan, who could not rely on being able to read the field guide each time they wanted to recall the information, carefully remembered all that Britt would tell them. This meant that later, when the information was wanted, Maggie and Dan had their knowledge with them, whereas Britt was dependent on having the field guide with her for the same information.

You may wonder if late reading makes it more difficult for a child to take in complex materials when he does begin to read. I have found that though Britt read at age 4 and Maggie at age 11, by age 12 both were reading the same material. Maggie has an easier time understanding what she reads now since she read at a later age and therefore never read anything she did not understand. It seems important that a child understands what he reads rather than just recognizing words. It makes me think of something Rosseau wrote in *Emile*, "Books teach us to talk about things we know nothing about." Many books written for young children to read to themselves are filled with informational material that is not very valuable to them. Because of this I've found that children might just as well wait until their understanding is such that the material they read can be assimilated and used. From the time they began reading, Maggie and Dan have always sought out books that were at their level of comprehension. Because they read later they never waded through books that were written so that children could read them regardless of the sense the words made or books that were merely meant to entertain. Their lives were so full of action and doing that the idea of being entertained by someone else's experiences never seemed to draw them. The same is true of their relationship with television.

A home schooler in Massachusetts, whose boy was a late reader, says that "reading is a tool for Ronnie now, as it would be for an adult. He likes to read the *Wall Street Journal* and other financial news and is writing to mining companies about stock." When my own children first begin reading on their own it is to glean information on some aspect of their daily life, usually information about an animal they are in charge of here on the farm. Maggie was nearly 11 when she began reading and when she did, she was able to easily get all the answers she needed to her sheep questions from the sheep reference books. Shortly after beginning to read, Maggie wrote her own article on sheep-raising for *The Mother Earth News*, (March/April, 1985). Daniel at twelve is just beginning to be able to read the reference books we have for his work with the chickens. Up until this time his understanding of poultry has come through working with them a great deal, close observation of the chickens, experimentation, modification, and recapitulation of the results. He now has a solid foundation for understanding what he reads in the poultry reference books. Dan recently sold an article on his bantams to *The Mother Earth News* (Jan/Feb, 1987).

My two younger boys, 8 and 10, do not read yet and I know that every year that passes gives them a chance to take in their world on a first hand basis. With no television and no reading, everything they do is experiential. They will have a solid base of experience to which they can add all the secondary information that comes into their lives as they grow older. As Abraham Maslow emphatically states, "There is no substitute for experience, none at all."

Basically, this is what the parents of late readers have to look forward to - a child who prefers experiencing the world themselves, rather than feeling satisfied by someone else's experiences in the world. In the words of a friend, educator, and writer, John Holt, "I never allow myself to forget that someone, somewhere, has to see or do something directly before it can be written about. I still learn a lot more by looking and listening and thinking about what I see and hear than I do by reading."

Another benefit of late reading is that the printed word does not become the omnipotent voice that is always right to someone who has spent a good part of his formative years without it. He will rely on his own experimentation and experiences. British essayist, William Hazlitt warns us what reading can become when he says, "It is seeing with the eyes of others, hearing with their ears, and pinning our faith on their understanding." A late reader has the benefit of taking the world in on his own for a number of years and so has great faith in his own experience.

One summer when working with a group of children I observed three twelve year olds preparing to plant a plum tree. I told the children they would need fractional amounts of manure, compost, topsoil, sand and gravel, and told them how to incorporate these ingredients into their planting. From a distance I saw the children discussing how to get the proper amounts of materials to the hole they had dug with the one wheelbarrow they had to use. While two of the children were arguing over the way to figure out the proportion of each material needed based on a formula they had read about in their math books, the non-reader of the group set out with the wheelbarrow and came back with the needed materials in their proper amounts. He later told me he had pictured the whole thing in his mind as I had been telling them how to do it. Instead of relying on elaborate formulas and other abstract information he got right down to the primary level of the task.

I was made aware of the benefits of this kind of first hand thinking recently when my eighteen year old was preparing potato soup for supper. Eight year old Jonah was assisting Britt and as they worked she would talk about the various ingredients she was using. She told him that she was adding her favorite herb, dill, to the soup as she reached for the jar labeled, "Dill" and began measuring it out. He told her it wasn't dill just as she was preparing to add it to the soup pot. He had tasted it and knew that no matter what abstraction was written on the jar, the reality was not dill. Jonah's habit of looking to the first hand experience rather than relying on secondary information saved our soup! Looking to first hand experience becomes a habit with children who are not yet readers.

One of the greatest benefits to a late reader may be the actual time he gains from not being able to sit for hours with a book. I remember when Dan was 10 and still a non-reader, he decided to build a raft for himself. Dan had been experimenting with the world first hand since he was born and had gleaned all kinds of information from his experience and his conversations with people around him. His action based life had also contributed to the motivated spirit he possesses - a necessary ingredient for putting one's dreams and ideas into action. He worked for two days putting his raft together and on the third day he varnished it and set it to dry. Meanwhile, his younger brothers, who'd been watching Dan and helping where they could, decided they would like a raft too. Dan tested the first raft on a neighbor's pond and then made the necessary modifications on the second raft for his brothers. By the time he finished the second raft, Maggie had decided to join her brothers on the rafting project and the four of them planned a trip down the creek. When they finally set out, two on each raft, they were prepared adventurers. A real adventure down the Doughty Creek on a beautiful spring day was the result of this ten year old's action. It brings to mind Abraham Maslow's words that there is a need in education "to teach the individual to examine reality directly and freshly" and that instruction has become more and more the study of "what other people have done rather than the doing itself." Later, when Dan had become a reader, he sat by the cozy stove on a cold winter evening and read about Huck Finn. He had real experiences upon which to hang the words of Mark Twain and his affinity with the adventurer in that tale was tremendous!

In several families I know where the children have acquired the tools of reading later, the reading in the family is often done by the parents. This not only enables the parents to select books that are uplifting and supportive of the family's values, but enables the family to make reading a time of togetherness; something unnecessary if everyone can read on his own and a great benefit for the late reader's entire family!

So if you find you have a seven or eight year old, or even an eleven or twelve year old not yet ready to read, relax and think of the benefits - there are a number of them, and there are many years ahead in which your child can be a reader.

From the November, 1987 issue of *Home Education Magazine.*

When Your Child Begins to Read

Sister Catharine Quinn

When parents approach me with the question, "How can I help my child to read?" my response is a simple one - "Ask yourself why you like to read." When you have answered this question you are on your way to helping your child. The answer, of course, is "I read for ideas." Whether the reading material be fact or fiction the reason for reading is in order to get in touch with the ideas that it contains.

Ideas come in all forms from the factual to the fictional depending upon the author's purpose. Words are the medium through which we get the message but words as words are never the goal of reading. It is important to keep this in mind when teaching a beginner to read because there is the temptation to focus attention on the unfamiliar words. Interrupting the flow of the story to "sound out" a word or ask for recall of a word can defeat the purpose and give the child a distaste for reading.

It is better to settle down with the book and let the child listen to the ideas. Whether it be reading the story of Tom Thumb or a book about dinosaurs, if the focus of reader and listener is on the ideas that the story contains, the story will compel the reader's attention. Teaching words can be done in a series of word games apart from the reading time.

One of the most important factors in good reading is rhythm. Every sentence has a certain rhythm and writers are aware of this rhythm in their writing. Who has not enjoyed the rhythmic chant of "Fee, fie, fo, fum, I smell the blood of an Englishman!" or "Trip, trap, trip, trap, across the bridge went the little Billy Goat Gruff." A de-emphasis on the words and a greater emphasis on the rhythm in sentences will make reading not only more intelligible to the child but more enjoyable, too.

The rhythm in Dr. Suess books is a good example of the great appeal rhythm has for children. Pick up one of these books and give yourself the pleasure of just riding-the-words as they flow along. You will respond and get the idea of what rhythmic reading as opposed to word-reading can do for the reader.

Up to this point, what I have written applies chiefly to the enjoyment of reading with your child: story-time, as it were, for you and your child. Now, I should like to suggest ways in which you can apply this theory to that important time when the young first or second grade level reader needs help. Again, keep in mind that even though this is a more formal approach to "learning how to read," the principle remains the same: the goal of reading is enjoyment of the ideas in the story - the storyline is paramount.

Approach the lesson in the same companionable attitude of discovering what this interesting story is all about. In order to do this, the adult must anticipate that the child will not be familiar with all the words in the story. Here is the stumbling block, mentioned above, where interrupting the storyline to concentrate on word attack skills can take all the enjoyment out of the reading lesson. Therefore, the few simple guidelines proposed here will help avoid this pitfall.

First, let the parent-helper assume most of the reading task. Begin by reading the story yourself, thus giving the child an example of the rhythm, voice-intonation and expression that makes the story meaningful and interesting to the reader. The child's part will be secondary to the enjoyment of listening. After the parent has started the oral reading with interest and expression, the child's part occurs by simply halting in the middle of every two or three sentences and asking the child to complete the sentence by reading it orally. This insures the child's attention and gives the necessary practice for reading on her own. By using this method the rhythm, tempo, and meaning are not interrupted, as is the case when a child is asked to do all the reading on her own. This pattern can prevail throughout the story and set the tone for the child to enjoy good oral reading instead of the tedium of hesitant word-by-word reading where concentration becomes focused on the unfamiliar words in the story, causing unnecessary difficulties. If the child stumbles on a word in her own part of the reading, say the word for her so the story doesn't lose its rhythm and meaning. Should she need help keeping her place in the story, use a bookmark above the sentence and move it down slowly while reading, but do not point to individual words. This keeps the emphasis on meaningful phrases and not words.

At what point in the preparation of the lesson does learning the vocabulary begin? This can best be accomplished at a time apart from the reading of the story itself through a series of word games. Children are highly motivated by games, and vocabulary building and word recognition skills lend themselves very well to this method of learning. Here are a few time tested effective suggestions, but more will occur to you as you work with these:

Word Families - Using colorful construction paper build ladders of words beginning with a basic root. Ask the child to think of all the words that can be formed by adding a single consonant to the root of these families: all, ball, call; and, band, sand; it, sit, pit; etc.

Sentence Building - On small 2" x 3" pieces of paper select words from the child's reader (example: kite, Jim, can, the, fly). Have the child arrange these in sentence order with variations (Jim can fly the kite. Can Jim fly the kite?).

Concentration - Again, select words from the basic reader and have the child print them on 2" x 3" pieces of paper. Show four of these words face-up (example: house, boat, with, sun). Ask the child to say the words and concentrate on their position. Now, turn them face-down and say each word and check the child's ability to locate it. Add more words as the child shows ease in ability to concentrate and locate.

Vocabulary Building - Show the child how new words can be formed by adding prefixes and suffixes (example: talk, talked, talking; safe, unsafe, safely).

Ask for Opposites - big, little; high, low; up, down.

Children love to draw pictures. Write names of objects in the picture and ask the child to label them: house, sun, tree, window, etc.

Attention span is important in the reading process. Never prolong the story or game beyond the child's interest. Several short periods are better than one long session. Keep as a rule-of-thumb that when either parent or child is tired, it's time to relax.

At all times let successful achievement and pleasure through learning be the goal of the time spent with your child. This will insure that reading is achieving its true purpose for parent and child, and you'll be rewarded with many more requests to "Read me a story, please?" or "Let's play a word game!"

From the May-June, 1988 issue of *Home Education Magazine.*

Serendipity in the Archives

Sue Smith-Heavenrich

It's a cold gray morning and no one wants to get dressed for breakfast. Instead, two pajama-clad children with books under their arms creep softly into the bedroom chanting "Read, Mommy, read!" While other children are shivering in the cold waiting for the schoolbus, we are snuggled under a warm quilt sharing adventure and discovery. Breakfast can wait, for now there are dragons to slay, oceans to cross, caves to explore.

Reading aloud is an important part of our homeschooling curriculum and our family time together. In the mornings it gives us time to wake up, to make the transition to a day full of activity and curious exploration. Afternoon storytime allows us a quiet interlude... time to lay down and listen, to renew ourselves. Throughout the day we turn to books to find answers to questions, perhaps reading about the purple finch we just identified at the feeder. Sometimes we just need a break from activity, and reading aloud gives us a shared time to learn together.

When people think of books for young children they often envision picture books. Yet when I look at the stacks of books we bring home from the library I find they are a wonderfully eclectic mixture of science and technology, math and biology, history, easy readers and story books. What is interesting is how often a book chosen purely by chance will open up a "unit of study." A few months ago my six-year-old son Coulter, who loves boats, pulled a rather large volume off the shelf for it's cover—a painting of an old sailing ship. "You know, it doesn't have many pictures," I remarked. Exhibiting inherited tenacity, he stuffed it in the already overflowing satchel with a look that left no doubt that this book was going home with us.

This particular book, *Carry On Mr. Bowditch*, by Jean Lee Latham, chronicles the life of Nathaniel Bowditch. It is full of sea lore, tales of privateers and pirates, ocean storms, shipwrecks, and mathematics. In addition to being a biography of one of America's brilliant navigators and mathematicians, it is the story of a self-educated scholar.

Nat is eager to learn, however, a combination of post-Revolutionary War politics and a depressed economy force him to leave school when he is ten. While making barrels in his father's workshop, Nat dreams of going to Harvard. While is mind is agile, Nat's hands are not. His father, faced with too many mouths to feed and diminishing economic resources, apprentices him to the Ship Chandlery as bookkeeper.

Curious and bright, Nat is fortunate to have been indentured to men who not only allow him the opportunity to continue learning, but encourage him. He is introduced to many helpful adults, some of whom become mentors, lending him books, discussing his questions, sharing their skills and knowledge. Nat fills notebook after notebook with observations on navigation, surveying, math and even Latin. He particularly loves numbers, and at the age of 15 discovers a way to predict moonrise and the tides, and sets to writing an almanac. In addition to geography and history, there are lessons in vocabulary (maritime lingo), how to calculate a ship's speed using a log, and latitude and longitude.

The stories are full of adventure, and they are real. Over the many days it took us to read we traced the ship's routes on our globe, studied atlases, located the meridian of Greenwich, and played with compasses. Coulter spent countless hours sailing to places with exotic names aboard his vessel, a piece of old porch deck out in the woods. He browsed through the "S" volume of World Book studying ships, and spent hours drawing different types of vessels, some real, some invented. We read up on the War of 1812, discussed the finer distinctions between being a "privateer" and being a "pirate," and checked Tchaikovsky's 1812 Overture out of the library. I probably couldn't have planned a unit of study like this if I'd tried!

This was not the first time a book has taken over our studies. Last year, as we read the biography of Louis Agassiz, we found ourselves dissecting a recently deceased pet goldfish. Perhaps this is one of the greatest advantages to learning outside of school, the freedom to go off on a tangent, to explore in depth a topic that piques our interest. The books we read have not undergone "educational censorship," they are not watered down readers with a limited vocabulary. Our books are real, rich in language and the complexities of life. It's true we often have to stop to define a word, discuss a phrase, chew over a topic. Unlike TV, we can mark a page, then go knead bread or ride a bike or dig for worms while we mull over things requiring more thought. Saint John's we're not, but we do have a great "books curriculum."

From the May-June, 1988 issue of *Home Education Magazine.*

Finding Reasons to Write

Earl Stevens

I put a piece of paper under my pillow, and when I could not sleep I wrote in the dark.   - Henry David Thoreau

Because I like to write, and because I spend lots of time doing it, parents and kids sometimes ask me questions about writing. "How does one learn to write?" they ask. "How does one become a writer?" They aren't asking how one becomes a world-famous novelist or poet or journalist, because I am none of those things. I think they are merely wondering how one becomes comfortable enough with the English language so that working with it can be satisfying and productive rather than frustrating and scary.

There are many reasons why parents are interested in making it possible for their kids to become good at writing. At the top of the list is their correct perception that someone who is in command of the English language is going to have a far easier time of managing life and finding things to do in this age of information. You can be ignorant of practically everything academic, but if you are good at reading and writing you have the power to make practically everything in the world accessible to you. On the other hand, if you are very weak in what the schools call "language skills" you may need to plan your life a lot more narrowly and carefully. As in the Arabian Nights, words do open doors.

Reading comes before writing. We know that people who don't read well are unlikely to write well. To take a step back, then, how does one make it easier for kids to become strong readers?

Many families have found that it all comes down to one simple idea: Provide an environment where books and other printed materials are lying about everywhere, and people are using them. After that one need only observe the following rule of thumb: Situations that discourage voluntary reading should be abandoned; situations that encourage voluntary reading should be nurtured. For instance, reading lots of interesting and amusing stories to enthusiastic kids is good. It demonstrates the value of reading. Forcing unwilling and resentful kids to sit through dull reading lessons is not so good. The lessons are about power and control, not about the joys of reading.

This is simple stuff that schools seem unable to comprehend, but parents can put it to use immediately. Learning to read is not very difficult and requires no special talent or preparation. It only requires a little support.

Assuming that a person is already an enthusiastic reader, then writing can be easily approached in the same non-violent manner. It is important to remember that learning how to draw neat letters on paper with a pen or pencil isn't necessarily "writing." It is penmanship. Many kids and adults find lengthy writing sessions with a pen or pencil to be cumbersome and laborious. Given a computer, a word processor, or a typewriter, they are far more likely to engage in lengthy writing projects. If we are convinced that early penmanship skills build character we can hand out calligraphy sets as birthday presents.

Like reading, writing is best learned in an environment which models and encourages it. If there are people around who engage in writing, and if there are obvious good reasons for kids to start to engage in writing, then they will do so. The parent who avoids much writing because of insecurity about his or her own writing skills can take the time to do something about it. The damage suffered during 12 years of English classes can be undone. What better time and place than now with one's own children.

Jamie taught himself to read over a long, comfortable period of time while listening to us read to him. Then, some years later, when he had the need to write, he became a person who writes. The catalyst for his writing was our subscription to a computer bulletin board service. (Hardware requirements: Any ordinary computer, a $99 modem, and a telephone. Your local computer fanatic will be glad to tell you about local and national online services.)

Once we set ourselves up on the service, writing suddenly became important for Jamie. He was sending and receiving electronic mail (E-mail), exchanging notes and letters with other kids and with adults all over the United States. He was in a sweat to send messages composed in standard English with a minimum of errors. He wanted to make a good impression. Don't we all? For two or three months he shouted out questions during sessions at the computer, mostly about spelling, sometimes about grammar. Without half realizing it, he also became a fast and accurate typist, and before long he became the fastest typist in the family. (It's always fun to do something better than your parents.)

People can learn to write without a computer (although there are lots of additional uses for them, and a modem will get you onto the "information superhighway" that everybody is talking about these days). The point is that what we did had nothing to do with lessons and workbooks and drills; it had everything to do with discovering good reasons for becoming a writer in the present instead of a would-be writer in some distant future.

I know the world is full of experts who say otherwise. They have written enough books to wallpaper the solar system. My opinion is that there is little need for experts and their methods. All that most kids need is an encouraging environment and a decent opportunity to discover for themselves, in their own time, the pleasures and the advantages of being a writer. Like reading, writing is not so much a basic skill but a way of life, one that is best learned casually, without commotion, while in pursuit of other interests.

From the March-April, 1994 issue of *Home Education Magazine.*

Reading Aloud

Michelle Delio

A little one snuggled on a parent's lap, contentedly listening to the rhythms of language as she is being introduced to the wonderful world of books. A group of young children gathered around a teacher, librarian or author, listening with rapt attention to the words of a book being brought to life. When we think of reading aloud it's always very little kids who populate the scene. Why do we deny our older kids, and ourselves, the special joy of being read to?

It seems that as soon as a kid is reading independently the amount of shared reading that a family does dwindles rapidly. Eventually it is reduced to inquiring if anyone has read a particular piece in that day's newspaper.

One of the gifts that homeschooling has given our family is the rediscovery of the fine art of reading aloud. It's one of the best ways I know to integrate two of the most important things in life; family and books.

Make no mistake, older kids love being read to. Grownups love being read to. Everyone, everywhere enjoys having the luxury of sitting back, closing their eyes and daydreaming their way into a book that's being read to them.

I rediscovered reading aloud when some of the books I really wanted to share with Devon were either above the level at which he felt comfortable reading, or books that he would not normally have chosen for himself. Rather than whining at him to "please read this, I loved it when I was your age," now I just read it to him. I get the joy of reexperiencing a childhood favorite, he gets to widen his circle of author friends. We both get to live within the covers of a good book for awhile.

Turn about is fair play and Devon enjoys reading some of the books he's discovered on his own to me. How else would I have learned about wonderful books such as the Magic Schoolbus series and Bunnicula, or renewed my acquaintance with authors I'd forgot such as Edward Eager, E. Nesbit and Susan Cooper?

Sometimes we use reading aloud as a way to encourage entry into a book with a writing style different from those my son is accustomed to. Reading two or three chapters together helps him become more comfortable with the author's style. Older books, particularly the "classics," are often written in a style that seems very dense to someone who is used to reading crisp modern prose. But a few shared chapters is often all it takes to immerse the kid in the story. The only problem with this method is that the book often disappears into the kid's room and you never get to hear the end of the story.

There is an art to reading aloud, and as with most arts, the more you do it the more proficient you become. Reading, or at least skimming, the book that you're going to be sharing before you begin reading it aloud is important. It will give you a feel for the author's style and the mood he or she is trying to set.

Reading aloud is performance art. But it's just you and your family, so have fun with it. Have a different voice for each of the story's characters. Vary your voice to show sadness, activity, confusion — whatever the plot indicates. Change your pitch, roar when a character yells, whisper, sing, whatever it takes to draw your listeners into the story. Interact with your listeners, if a story's character grips someone's arm, jumps out and scares them, pokes them, or hugs them, you can grab, scare, poke, and hug your kids.

Consider how the book you're reading can involve all of your kids senses. You can play a tape of ocean music for a book that's set on an island, or utilize some other appropriate sound effects. Pull down the blinds and light a candle for a spooky story. Read books about the great outdoors outside. Was your book made into a movie? Watch it after you finish reading. Is your book set in a location that you can visit? All of these activities help make reading the special event it is and extend the enjoyment of a good book.

Sharing a book makes for better conversations about books. Don't quiz your kids about what you're reading, but make sure they understand the meanings of key words. Talking about books is not asking "did you like that?" Talking about books is like chatting with a friend about another friend. When you've finished the book you can also talk about what the author did that made the book good or not so good. Explaining the techniques of good writing to kids: exciting leads, descriptive words, plot and pacing, how each chapter ends on a note that is intended to pull you into the next chapter — is a wonderful way to teach kids about effective writing. Don't worry about the formal terms for all this, just talk about what you liked and why you liked it. Mark pages that have particularly wonderful paragraphs and go back and figure out why they affected you. Professional writers use other author's books as their inspiration and education. You can too.

And just because it's in a book doesn't mean its perfect. Proofreaders and editors have their bad days, especially when they're working with an author who has written a few best selling books. Talk about how the book could have been better, how you would have changed it if you had been the author or editor. Then write a different ending.

Remember also that some stories were designed to be read aloud and are much more effective when you hear them spoken than when you read them silently. African folktales, Native American legends — anything that was important enough to memorize and be passed down for generations before being committed to paper should be read aloud, even if only to yourself. Check out the wonderful "Keepers" series of books by Michael Caduto and Joseph Bruchac. There are three books in the collection: *Keepers of the Earth, Keepers of the Animals,* and *Keepers of the Night.* Each book contains stories to read aloud, more than enough information about the natural world to be the foundation of any science program, and activities to do with the kids. They'd work for folks whose ages range from eight to grownup. I can't recommend them highly enough. The first two books have a teacher's guide (which is way less obnoxious than most teacher's guides and actually useful), but you can work with the books without the guides.

Beware though — there are certain repercussions to reading aloud. Hours will slip by and chores will not be done. Your voice will become hoarse and still you'll press on.

And your kids may decide that they love books!

From the July-August, 1994 issue of *Home Education Magazine*.

A Case for the Classics

Shari Henry

I sit legs crossed, Phoebe smooshed into my lap. My arms wrap around her as my hands clasp a copy of Mother Goose in front of us. She studies, points, and squeals, occasionally looking at me inquisitioning, "Eh, eh, eh?" I usually know what answer to give. As most toddlers, she understands more than most people would guess as we read through delicious rhymes about Jack and Jill, Little Boy Blue, and Old Mother Hubbard. Memories wash over me; memories of my grandma's voice reading the same rhymes to me years ago.

Eventually, muffins need to be baked, dishes washed, and laundry folded, spurring us to break up our reading party. Later, while Bekah and Phoebe drift off together to some faraway world in long skirts, scarves, and tiaras, TJ and I grab Robert Lawson's *Mr. Revere And I*, seize our spots on the couch, and dive into revolutionary life. Written in 1953, *Mr. Revere And I* doesn't condescend to children, but expects them to be able to "get it" - "it" being an interesting and somewhat complex story line, and loads of words no one ever uses anymore. Lawson will introduce a new word, for example, "impudent," then use it two or three more times over a few pages. Naturally, kids pick up the word's meaning. Here's the way he describes a large group of people gathering one day to protest the King's taxes: "Like a dark river the crowd from the mass meeting began to flow down the streets leading to the wharves." TJ and I could see that crowd!

Historical fiction happens to be our favorite genre. Aside from filling our minds with great literature and tidbits of history, we're reminded of the incredible legacy we've been given as Americans. The dedicated men and women, their sacrifices, their incomparable devotion to liberty. We ponder over the last thought a bit, wondering aloud what liberty means in 20th Century America. Does anyone care about preserving it? Our discussion could go on forever, but the girls understandably are ready for us to join them once again.

Lucky me. An hour or so later, Phoebe naps and Bek and I plunge into bed and pull the purple striped comforter up under our chins. We move through delightful treats about a duck named Ping, a girl named Madeline, and a snow shovel named Katy. We snuggle with Jemima Puddleduck, Peter Rabbit, and the sly fox, entering the world of luscious British phrases and higher respect for children's capabilities. Words like "soporific," "superfluous," and "alighted" sprinkle the pages.

Reading is a big part of our lives and we take it seriously. I read to my kids in part to give them a strong foundation for reading independently someday. Opening the pages of a book, the world comes to us: history, science, math, social studies, God's rules and plans, fantastic tales of imagination. The richer the language and higher quality the literature, the more we all enjoy our time together. No one should underestimate the significance of time parents spend reading with their children. No matter how stormy a day, the seas calm as we curl up together, focused on the pages in front of us. We all agree the best of times are made by sharing books.

Unfortunately, rather than seeing these kinds of books as challenging in a healthy way, many modern day authors and educational experts think of them as too difficult. Nowadays, books are written with more concern for political correctness than truth or style, and inane readers seem to procreate, providing easy learning material for children who may be better off waiting a few years to read. Top that off with horror stories and other themes which undermine society's commonly held values, and the vast majority of what lines children's library shelves belongs in the dumpster out back.

Educators, particularly reading specialists, encourage these trends, especially when working with Learning Disabled students. The theory goes that reading anything is better than not reading at all. If children struggle, give them blood-splattered comic books or silly tales about a gaggle of babysitters. According to this line of thinking, children should read whatever; it's reading that's important. This rationale only makes sense for a moment. Apparently it doesn't occur to experts that simplistic, non-edifying nonsense can't satisfy anyone's appetite for literature and certainly doesn't offer any long-term appreciation of where reading can take the reader.

Reading can and should nourish the mind, even the soul, in the same way food nourishes the body. Good food builds a strong body, good books a strong mind. Over time, children will learn to eat and love wholesome foods, but only if junk isn't too easily available.

I monitor my children's reading materials fervently. Fortunately, healthful reading materials are easy to promote because in fact, the nutritious is always more tasty. Read something by the Bearanstains, then something by Ingri and Edgar Parin d'Aulaire. Compare for yourself.

None of this is to say I never allow snacking on frivolous reading, but fun doesn't have to be completely void of value. A hungry child can eat a wholesome meal and still have room and time for a dish of ice cream. However, high quality books number too many to count. There simply isn't time to digest all the good stuff, much less make room for the junk.

By seeking out treasures, every subject area which interests families can be tackled easily, pleasurably. Textbooks become unnecessary, mundane books, useless. Good books are more fun! Watch as children become engrossed in stories about an elephant named Babar or a young Benjamin Franklin. They'll never be willing to settle for less quality. Best of all, books are one commodity where high quality isn't equaled by high prices. They're free at the local library.

Getting started is as exciting as it is challenging. Look for books you loved as a child, talk to friends, browse through resources such as *Books Children Love* by Elizabeth Wilson, *The New Read Aloud Handbook* by Jim Trelease, or *Honey For A Child's Heart* by Gladys Hunt, among others. Resource books vary in topics they address but certain titles and authors will pop up again and again. As we've familiarized ourselves with literary giants, we've noticed certain illustrators go hand-in-hand. N.C. Wyeth, Garth Williams, and Jessie Wilcox Smith didn't waste their lovely drawings on less than superb literature. Take notes and head to the library.

No matter how highly acclaimed a title, don't hesitate to ditch it if your kids don't like the book. It may not be the right time, or it may never be. It seems, for example, many girls fall in love with horses and devour every horse story ever written, among them *Black Beauty*, *The Black Stallion*, and *Misty Of Chincoteague*. All are great literature, but we've never read past the first chapter in any of them in our house. On the other hand, our dog-loving clan relished *Lassie*, *Sounder*, and *Where The Red Fern Grows*. There's so much great stuff out there we can't get to it all anyway. Choosing to read just the books we like helps us narrow the field and in no way compromises the kids' learning.

Be prepared for many titles to be out of print. A nearby library may still have some, , but don't overlook the obvious. Upon packing up our childhood home, my mother tossed books into boxes and set them in the corner of the basement to be picked up by Goodwill. Luckily, I was visiting and spent hours poring through eight children's worth of books. We've elbowed our way through library book sales, dug in bottomless boxes at garage sales, and browsed disorganized shelves at Salvation Army for bargains galore. Used book stores are a reliable source, but the prices of older books begin to climb, especially if the owner knows the value of an out-of-print edition (many don't when it comes to children's literature). As a last resort, request a book search, but be prepared to pay a premium. Like anything else in life, set priorities and decide how much work you want to put into finding certain titles and how much you're willing to pay for the services of others.

I enjoy the thrill of the hunt when it comes to books. I often come home with two or three copies of the same title if I know others will want it, and phone likeminded friends to brag about my finds. A used book store once had a half dozen brand new copies of Catherine Vos's *A Child's Story Bible* priced at less than 1/4 of the suggested retail amount. Though the title isn't out of print, it's our favorite story *Bible* and I knew many friends had it on their wish lists. I purchased all the copies and sold them while running errands on my way home that afternoon!

Wherever or however you find the books, enjoy them. Unplug the phone or turn on the answering machine. We enjoy escaping on the magic carpet ride for journeys to remote places and distant times, real or imagined. Cozied up under blankets and against piled-high pillows, reading becomes our refuge from an all too busy world just outside our front door. May it do at least as much for you.

From the September-October, 1994 issue of *Home Education Magazine*.

MATH/ SCIENCE

Part Three - Subjects One Two Three

Teaching the Sciences

John Holt

John Holt wrote to a parent: With respect to your question of how a parent could teach a subject like chemistry, there seem to be a number of possibilities, all of which people have actually done in one place or another. 1. The parent finds a textbook, materials, etc., and parent and child learn the stuff together. 2. The parents get the above for the child, and the child learns it alone. 3. The parent finds, or the child finds, someone else, perhaps a teacher in some kind of school, or even college, who knows this material, and learns it from them.

As for equipment, you say that your high school had a very extensive chemistry lab, but I'll bet that very few of the students ever used more than a small part of the materials in the lab. I have known kids who were interested in chemistry and did it in their own basements, who were able to do a great deal of work with, at today's prices, less than $200 or maybe $100 worth of equipment. The catalog of Edmund Scientific Corporation (101 E. Gloucester Park, Barrington, NJ 08007) is full of such equipment. Same thing is true of physics. As for biology, except perhaps in the heart of the city, it is not difficult to find animals for examination, dissection, etc. if that is what your children want to do. I won't say there are not problems, but people who want to solve them can solve them.

You ask, "Would you expect a parent to purchase test tubes, chemicals, instruments, etc., that would perhaps only be used for one or two years, only to have the child become an artist or musician?" Well, why not? People purchase bicycles, sports equipment, musical instruments, without knowing that their children will ever become professional athletes, musicians, etc. None of this equipment (unless broken) loses any of it's value — it could probably be sold later for at least a significant part of the purchase price.

I see no real need for "institutional" education at any age. There is a man named Ovshinsky, in Michigan, who stood physics on its ear by inventing a theory by which non-crystalline substances could be used to do things which, according to orthodox theory, only crystalline materials could do. For a number of years orthodox physicists dismissed Ovshinsky's ideas. But he was able to demonstrate them so clearly in laboratory experiments that they were finally obliged to admit that he was right. But he never finished high school! There are probably more cases like this than we know, and there would be a great many more except for compulsory schooling laws. It is a kind of Catch 22 situation to say, first, that all children have to spend all that time in schools, and then to say that all kinds of things can be learned only in schools. How do we know? Where have we given people a chance to learn them somewhere else?

A very important function of institutions of so-called higher learning is not so much to teach people things as to limit access to certain kinds of learning and work. The function of law school is much less to train lawyers than to keep down the supply of lawyers. Practically everything that is now done only by people with Ph. D's was, not so very long ago, done by people with no graduate training or, in some cases, even undergraduate training. Schools do not create much learning. What they mostly do is collect it, hoard it, and sell it at the highest possible prices.

I hope you will not doubt your competence to help your children learn anything they want to learn, or indeed their competence to learn many things without your help.

From the January, 1986 issue of *Home Education Magazine.*

Hands-On-Science

Sue Smith Heavenrich

Children are, by nature, scientists. They are eager to find out how something works, and will spend hours patiently taking apart all the alarm clocks in the house (given a chance). Unfortunately, science education seems to discourage learning. There is too much content to cover to meet course requirements, and too little time for lab and field studies. Especially in the lower grades, textbooks tend to avoid the use of sophisticated language and seem dumbed-down. Often the information is over-simplified and broken into sequential bits - neat if you're organizing an outline, but maybe not the way some scientifically-minded children want their information. Mine, for example, want theirs in huge gulps, long words and all.

Scientific discovery implies taking risks - doing an investigation to "find out." Risks sometimes lead nowhere, and in normal science courses there is no time to redesign experiments. Because risk-taking requires making allowances for "failure," and because failure is punished in our schooling society, there is little encouragement for students to do creative science.

If we want to raise scientifically literate, inventive thinkers, we must change the way science is learned. We need to create an environment that allows for discovery. For children this means making tools and equipment accessible, and having a place to do messy experiments. We need to eliminate the need to "ask for permission" if we truly want our children to investigate their own questions. This was made clear to me a couple of years ago when my children and their young cousin decided to explore the properties of magnetism. While I was getting breakfast together, these 2- to 5-year old investigators were busy rummaging through the desk drawers and cupboard collecting all the necessary gear. When I peeked around the corner, I found them seriously studying the effects of magnets on compasses. This could not have happened if they'd needed me to get things for them - it was a spontaneous experiment designed to answer a question important to them at that point in time.

Hands-on discovery can get messy, and children need to know that it's okay to get the table or floor wet. It is by "messing around" that we find new avenues for investigation. Maybe we've been doing paper chromatography using markers and food dye, and we decide to try adding acids or bases to the water. There's bound to be spills, and worry about keeping things clean can really inhibit young investigators. Another worry is that things you try "won't work." If we can allow ourselves to try experiments without having to know the outcome, we will feel freer to risk discovery.

You can't shortcut the natural process of discovery. What may appear to an adult as repetitive play may in reality be testing and refinement of a theory. A few year ago *Growing Without Schooling* (#47) printed a short article describing one boy's investigations using a balance. He put 16 bottle caps on one side, then a number on the other. He worked with the bottle caps for about three and a half hours convincing himself that 16 on one side would balance 16 on the other. Once convinced, he quickly went on to confirm that 6 wooden cubes balanced 6 wooden cubes, and 12 marbles, 12 marbles.

Traditional science instruction may interfere with this process by substituting textbook reading for actual discovery. This is why hands-on science activities are so important - they provide the vehicle for the child to make his own discoveries. Keep science investigations open-ended and leave experiments set up awhile to encourage further play.

Probably the most important part of helping your child learn science is to be willing, yourself, to test uncharted waters. It is okay to not know the answer! This allows you to say, "I don't know. Let's find out." I am reminded of a friend's daughter who decided to return to school when she was in 8th grade. She was so excited because the science room was full of things to use. But her excitement quickly faded. "There is no wonder," she told me. "We do the labs but they are busy-work labs. The teacher doesn't allow us to ask questions. He's afraid he won't know the answer."

Doing Science

Science often comes from observing the world and asking questions. "What's inside these old acorns?" "What will hatch from this egg sac?" "What sort of seeds do birds prefer?" "How far does a pickerel frog travel in one leap?" These are the sorts of questions that lead so naturally to collecting information (data), designing tests, and analyzing results.

Scientific inquiry should include fair tests and lead to valid results. One can learn a lot from informal anecdotal stories, but if you want to pursue a question as a scientist might, then you need to take the time to design an experiment. You need to consider: Is our experiment (test) fair? Are we testing only one thing at a time (perhaps the effect of color of light on plant growth). Do we have enough of a sample size to make any prediction? Usually it takes about 40 tests or observations to be able to state results with an amount of certainty. For example, if your child notices that there are some larvae in an old acorn he's cracked open, you can suggest collecting a lot more and seeing if they have larvae too.

Try to ask questions that can be answered by counting things. This makes collecting the data easier, and you can subject your subjects to a statistical analysis. That means you can graph them, chart them, or even do simple statistics.

An important thing to keep in mind is not to let hasty conclusions

bias your observations. This is especially important if you are studying animal behavior, perhaps watching beetles on a milkweed plant. A
child may observe one beetle climbing on another beetle's back and
waving it's antennae around in an agitated way. If he calls this behavior an "attack," he then colors his subsequent observations and may
miss learning that it was really a courtship behavior.

Scientists are often pictured working in labs, surrounded by shelves
of glassware and chemicals. But you can do a lot with a notebook, a
pencil, and a stopwatch. One of my favorite investigations happened
during a bicycle ride. "Why is it," my son wondered, "that I have to
pedal twice as much to go the same distance as you?"

"Let's look at the bikes," I suggested. We began by comparing tire
sizes, reading the diameter measurements printed on their sides. Then
I drew a starting line in the dirt and we lined up our bicycles. We
rolled each bike one tire-revolution forward and marked the distance
travelled with a stick. When we were finished we had a visual repre-
sentation, a crude "bar graph" that showed us something about the
relationship between diameter and distance travelled. We hopped
back on our bikes to finish our ride, and I thought the investigation
was finished. Not so! The minute we got home my son grabbed the
bike repair manual. He'd noticed my caliper brakes and gears, and
wanted to know about them, too.

This brings up an important point: If it's real, it's worth studying.
Questions that come out of a child's experiences lead to investigations
with results that have personal meaning. Real science has value, and
the answers add to our understanding of our world. Unfortunately,
too much of the science found in textbooks is "busywork." One year,
when the Gypsy moths were so bad you could hear them munching
the forest, my son asked, "How much does a Gypsy moth eat?" Not
hard to figure out really... just capture a few and put them into jars,
and give them a leaf or two. We made tracings of the leaves, planning
to compare eaten leaves with their original tracings and see the area of
leaf consumed. An interesting thing happened though. The next day
when we retrieved the leaves from the jars, we noticed they'd all been
cut in half. Had the leaves been on a tree, the cut part would fall to
the ground uneaten. This explained why there were bits of leaves all
over the ground outside, and how the larvae could defoliate the trees
so quickly.

One thing necessary to learning is having time to digest the information. If you do a short experiment and it doesn't seem to generate

lots of discussion, wait a bit. Maybe around dinner time you'll hear your children talking it over, trying the experiment again on their own. It might be the sort of thing that needs to rattle around inside their heads a bit, but a week later they'll surprise you with questions that will send you to the reference section of your library.

Remember to take time to analyze and discuss your results. Making graphs is a fun activity, and a good way to condense lots of information so you can refer to it later on. If you want to tie in math, then explore "means" and "ranges" (for example, the average distance travelled by caterpillars in one minute), or for older students see if you can do a Chi-Square test. Just don't let your calculations get so out of hand that you forget your initial reason for doing the project: to answer a question, to learn, to have fun.

Meeting the Science Requirements

When we wrote up our curriculum plan for the year, we kept it simple and open-ended. Our science instruction encourages a hands-on approach, emphasizing the interconnectedness between physical and biological sciences. Our children are active participants in designing experiments, collecting data, and analyzing the results. We depend primarily on observation and experimentation, go on lots of field trips, and supplement the hands-on studies with reading. We did not list topics to be studied because we do not know what direction our interests will take.

A great advantage of homeschooling science is the freedom to capitalize on current interests. We can study electricity when our child raises the topic, rather than waiting until it's covered in the curriculum. But what does one do if no one wants to do science? This does sometimes happen.... maybe knights in armor is all your child wants to study. If you feel that you really must do something, then find something you want to do. Gather the material, sit at the children's work table, and begin to experiment. Most likely your reluctant scientists will drift over to see what you're up to. Then as you continue your investigation you can explain the details, offering the children opportunities to help. If you're using salt and vinegar to turn tarnished pennies shiny (from *The Backyard Scientist* series), you might tie it in with a discussion on how knights cleaned their armor.

Make science interdisciplinary. There are some good science stories that you can use for reading time, and collecting and analyzing data bring you into the realm of mathematics. If your question touches on the relationship of humans with the environment or each other you have a tie in with social studies. Sound and color experiments combine with music and art.

The amount of time we spend "doing science" fluctuates each week and depends upon the seasons. We might spend an hour in the garden watching bees or digging for soil critters, or 15 minutes observing birds at the feeder. The National Science Teachers Association recommends a minimum of one and one-half hours per week in grades K-3, and two and one-half hours per week in grades 4-6. Though it's not a lot of time, even 20 minutes a day can be a lot of science if the time is devoted to actually doing an investigation.

Whatever your style or inclination, there are a number of inquiry skills that should be included in your science activities. They include: classifying (sorting things into groups using a system); creating models (graphs, diagrams, charts, 3-D models, photographs); formulating hypotheses; generalizing (drawing conclusions); identifying variables (factors that would influence your study); inference; making decisions; interpreting data; manipulating materials (using the tools of scientific study); measuring; observing (using the senses to predict as much as you can); predicting; recording data; replicating (duplicate someone else's experiment or procedure to see if you get the same results); and using numbers.

At the elementary and middle school level, science combines the study of the physical world and life sciences. There are lots of everyday activities that involve science in some way. Growing a garden, cooking, keeping track of rainfall, or going on nature walks are just a few of them. Or take a field trip - a visit to the zoo, planetarium, museum, or local nursery. Include reading biographies of scientists and inventors. Hearing about real people often makes science come alive for children, and may spur them on to investigate something new. Though most encyclopedias and books focus on well known male scientists and inventors, there are many women, blacks, Hispanics, and Native Americans who have contributed to our understanding of how the world works.

From the January-February, 1994 issue of *Home Education Magazine*.

Magic Math Solutions

Becky Rupp

Randy - my husband - and I spread all our math materials out on the bed a few nights back and pored over them, in an attempt to evaluate, update, revamp, or trash our current mathematics program. Math methods, in our house, tend to rise and fall like banana republics. I keep hoping, I think, to find the Magic Math Solution - some program or technique that will have the boys popping out of their bunks in the morning, eager for arithmetic. They're eager for almost everything else. "Let's do chemistry experiments!" they'll say, or "Let's finish *The Borrowers!*" Let's build a model log cabin! Let's play the map game again!" Mention math, though, and it's as if the hawk just passed over the cheeping sparrows. Somewhere we've gone wrong.

What we've got here, after six years of expensive floundering, is a math collection of truly appalling size. We have Cuisenaire rods, Unifix cubes, lots of play money in various denominations, and a blue and yellow plastic arm balance with (most of) the blue plastic 1 gram hanging weights. We have two trays worth of Mortensen manipulatives, plus Mortensen workbooks; we have Miquon workbooks, in Orange, Red, Blue, Green, Yellow, and Purple; and we just acquired our first math textbook, *Math 54*, by Stephen Hake and John Saxon. We have a kitchen scale picked up at a flea market, an assortment of rulers and measuring tapes, at least three working calculators, two thermometers, a stopwatch, and a lot of clocks, two with second hands. We have one child who tolerates math, one who loathes it, and one who maintains a cautious neutrality. We have no Magic Math Solution. We do, however, have a few ideas.

Cuisenaire rods. Cuisenaire rods are by far the most attractive math manipulatives we've seen. They're richly colorful and made of solid wood; they look good and they feel good. All our kids like playing with them, building with them, fooling around with them. In our hands, however, they have not been successful as math aids. The drawback of the Cuisenaire rods is that they are not scored. You can't, for example, look at a Cuisenaire six-bar and know right off that the thing is a six-bar. No little lines.

The Mortensen manipulatives aren't as handsome, but they're definitely our pick. They are made of colored plastic, scored on one side, blank on the others. They come in all the same sizes as Cuisenaire rods, plus some - the Mortensen kit, for example, includes 100-squares. We've found them endlessly versatile and we use them constantly. Unfortunately the accompanying Mortensen workbooks are totally ugly - blah little newsprint booklets - and tend to be grindingly repetitive. Some of their methodology seems a bit convoluted to me, but it doesn't seem to bother the kids, who do move smoothly, but unenthusiastically, through the Mortensen program.

The Miquon workbooks are our favorite math workbooks to date - they're pretty, they're clever, and they have more of a puzzle feel to them than a problem feel, which is very appealing. They are the only math workbooks I've yet seen that really seem to promote creative thinking and problem solving skills, rather than rote performance. Drawback: they only go through (Purple) third grade. They're designed for use with the Cuisenaire rods, but we've found that except in a few odd cases they adapt perfectly well to the Mortensen manipulatives.

And now there are the new kids on our mathematical block: Stephen Hake and John Saxon, whose publications are no-nonsense solid worth. The Hake/Saxon math program is solid meat and potatoes arithmetic, the stuff I remember from Chambers Elementary School. Their examples are absolutely clear, but unexciting. It's not cute, but it's thorough. There are some K-1 level workbooks available, but other than that, unfortunately, the lowest level Hake/Saxon textbook currently on the market is *Math 54*, recommended for fifth graders and advanced fourth graders. It looks about right for our almost ten-year-old, the math hater. If we can coax him to work through it, he'll have fifth grade math down, but it's not going to make him a math lover. There's something to be said for this, as far as it goes, but there's something to be said against it, too.

Our home math picture, for all my gloomy griping, isn't totally grim. We've had good luck with mathematically oriented books. The boys have all adored the Mitsumasa Anno books: *Anno's Counting House, Anno's Hat Tricks, Anno's Math Games, Anno's Math Games II,* and *Anno's Mysterious Multiplying Jar.* The mysterious jar, which introduces the concept of factorials, was particularly appealing to our bunch. They read and re-read it, invented puzzles based on it, and Joshua wrote a book of his own based on it, having done so with mysterious multiplying pens. Glory St. John's *How to Count Like a Martian* - or like a Babylonian, ancient Egyptian, or Roman - was fairly popular; and everybody liked *The King's Chessboard* (David Birch) which is a retelling of an old story in which the king promises to give a wise man one grain of rice for the first square on the chessboard, two grains for the second, four grains for the third, then eight grains, then sixteen - until somewhere in the middle of the chessboard the king realizes his terrible mathematical mistake.

David Schwartz's *How Much is a Million?* and *If You Made a Million* were both wonderful; and *The Phantom Tollbooth* (Norton Juster) is mathematically (and otherwise) priceless. *The Money* volume in the *Eyewitness Books* series (Alfred A. Knopf) is a beauty, stuffed with exquisite color photographs; it covers all things monetary from the cowrie shell to the credit card. Thomas Y. Crowell publishes a series of elementary-level children's books about various math concepts - for example, *Angles Are Easy as Pie* and *What Do You Mean By Average?* - which have whipped up mild interest. The only one of the series that really sparked them off, though, was a little book on negative numbers, titled *Less Than Nothing Is Really Something*. This simply fascinated them. We read the book several times, and it plunged into long discussions on the freezing point, the workings of thermometers, the difference between warm- and cold-blooded animals, frostbite, hypothermia, mountain-climbing, the height of Mt. Everest, the depth of the Mariana Trench, and survival in the Antarctic.

Joshua, our nearly ten-year-old, likes *The I Hate Mathematics! Book* and *Math for Smarty Pants* - they're both in the Brown Paper School book series, written by Marilyn Burns and published by Little, Brown and Company. *The I Hate Mathematics! Book* gets off on the right foot: "Some of the nicest people hate mathematics. Especially kids who think mathematics = arithmetic." ("This book," said Josh, "is for ME.") The books are creative and delightful: lots of (hands-on) puzzles and mind-benders. It's *not* arithmetic; these books are an entrancing introduction to real mathematics. Concepts covered include topology, prime numbers, binary numbers, infinity, "The Preposterous Googol," the parabola. Our younger kids have enjoyed some of the puzzles, but the books in their entirety have only caught on so far with Josh. They look to me about right for the 9-11 age group.

Then there are math games. One success in our home has been a geometry game called *O! Euclid!* It's subtitled "An Amusing and Scholarly Card Game for Ages 9-99," but in my experience four-year-olds can handle it just fine. It involves putting together puzzle pieces to make a variety of geometric shapes, from the simple (square) to the not-so-simple (trapezoid, hyperbola). Less successful were *Math Trivial Pursuit* (I had to bribe them) and *Math-It*. *Math Trivial Pursuit* (Good Apple) is available in primary and intermediate levels: our version came in paperback book format. There's a folded playing board included, lots and lots of question cards (which have to be cut out) and a little box to keep them in (which has to be assembled). You provide your own playing pieces and dice. Nice solid math questions in four categories, with enough range in complexity that the game can be played by kids of several different ages all at once.

Math-It is basically a memory math game; it's designed to help kids learn arithmetic facts, using problem cards and an answer board. There's a *Pre-Math-It* version, using dominoes. The boys have used both, and they work - but work better when the user is motivated to master the principles involved. Everybody had fun playing with Mama and the dominoes, but *Math-It* - face it - was memorizing arithmetic, and our gang immediately pegged it as such, a mathematical wolf in game clothing. I haven't given up on *Math-It*; I am biding my time and waiting for motivation.

Computer games are winners with practically every child we know, but our two oldest are lukewarm about computerized math, even when beeping dancing rabbits celebrate the right answer. Caleb, our six-year-old, is a different story: he dearly loves computer games. We have two math games, both well-recommended: *Math Rabbit* (The Learning Company) and *Math Blaster* (Davidson). Both are conceptually pretty straightforward: you add, subtract, multiply or divide things correctly, and trains chug away, rabbits dance, or rockets blast off.

Math winners: some years ago, on a museum expedition in San Francisco, we acquired a "Path to Math" kit. It consists of a series of colored cardboard squares (ones, fives, tens, fifties, and one hundreds) and a pack of dice, both the conventional spotted cubes and those weird numbered polygonal models used in *Dungeons and Dragons*. Accompanying instructions explain how to play a number of tile-trading games, using various kinds of mathematical manipulations. Our children have loved this, have played it repeatedly, and have noticeably picked up some useful mathematical abilities from it. Everybody, for example, learned (painlessly) how to double numbers while tile-trading.

Another sure-fire math game at our house is a purely homemade buying and selling game. It consists of an ever-growing pack of tatty index cards, each with a picture drawn on it - castles, unicorns, giraffes, ice cream sundaes, magic wands, roller skates - and a price written underneath the picture. The kids pass out standard sums of paper money and we proceed to buy, sell, trade, and make change. I notice there are a couple of buy-and-sell type games on the market now, but I can't imagine a better (or cheaper) version than our home-made variety. Besides, I'll bet no professional hands out AMOEBA cards ($1.75) - and in our house you can purchase the entire solar system for a flat $7.32. I have an idea for a variation on this, using imaginary bank accounts and books of discarded checks. Maybe next year.

An audiovisual math hit around here is a Disney videotape called *Donald in Mathemagic Land*, which we all found delightful. It starts with the ancient Greeks and ends up demonstrating the mathematical aspects of cathedrals, baseball diamonds, starfish, and the Mona Lisa. We've also enjoyed *Square One*, a 30-minute math program on our public television station.

For grown-ups, Marilyn Burns and Bonnie Tank have written *A Collection of Math Lessons* (Math Solution Publications). There are two of these, the first covers grades 1 through 3, the second grades 3 through 6. There are many inventive ideas, for example, we all liked the probability experiments that involved making a "peek box," then estimating the numbers of different colored marbles contained in it - but the lessons are designed for kids in captive school groups, and are not at all successful at home. We found the same with *Family Math* (Jean Stenmark, Virginia Thompson, and Ruth Cossey), an enormous volume of math activities that has been highly recommended by educators. Some of the activities have caught interest around here, but equal numbers have flopped. (Our kids can recognize sugar-coated arithmetic at fifty paces.) *Family Math* has been a useful resource for us, the parents: it's got a nice list in the back of which math skills are generally required by the public schools at each grade level through grade 6; and it's a wonderful source for copying hundred charts, number lines, graph paper in various grid sizes, and blank calendars.

It includes a buying and selling game. You get to buy pencils and band-aids.

While I've been typing this, the boys, armed with metal measuring tapes, have been trotting around the house measuring doorways, trying to figure out if Abraham Lincoln could have passed from room to room in here without bending his knees. (No.) That's math. Not the

Magic Math Solution, perhaps, but on days like this I feel like we're headed in the right direction.

From the May-June, 1991 issue of *Home Education Magazine*.

How One Mother Inspires Her Kids in a Subject She Hated

Aneeta Brown

I dropped out of arithmetic in the sixth grade, defeated and discouraged by my inability to divide decimals. I barely passed required ninth grade algebra, received my first (and only) D in sophomore geometry, managed to earn a college degree without ever taking a math course, and today consider my checkbook " in balance" if the amount is within five dollars of the bank statement.

Fortunately, children don't "inherit" all the mental weaknesses of their parents. I believe that a zeal for learning can have a profound impact on a child's attitude about the value of math. What a gift! Because we play so many games with our children, they're learning basic math skills that will reduce their stress and frustration throughout their lives.

We're confident they'll be able to master, by age 12, the following tasks with pencil and paper, or brainpower alone:

Mentally doublecheck the math on a handwritten restaurant check;

Halve the ingredients in a recipe;

Converse intelligently with a lumberyard clerk while discussing measurements for a project;

Determine the amount of money due them after a sales transaction;

Calculate simple interest on a savings account;

Read a road map and estimate some mileage;

Understand the concept of unit pricing.

From our game closet, the kids are becoming proficient in math with the choices they make. With *Battleship*, they've learned how to read a grid. With *Monopoly*, how to count paper money as well as how to estimate income, expenses, and losses. *Clue* has given them deductive reasoning skills, and *Checkers* and *Chess* show them there's more than one way to solve a problem. *Dutch Blitz* is a lively card game with complex scoring that challenges their best addition and subtraction skills. And they don't realize it yet, but *Gin Rummy* contains examples of set theory that they'll encounter in algebra someday.

A couple of years ago we taught our boys to play the card game *Hearts*. Our youngest, then six, needed a full year to master the dealing, sorting, and handling functions (we're still working on the shuffling), but what a crowd pleaser the game has been. We play with friends and families of all ages, including the boys' four grandparents. Each has a half-century of card-playing experience, but sometimes the kids do win. My husband maintains that if a third-grader can conceptualize that a Jack, for example, has a higher value than the 10 spot, that same youngster can, in years ahead, probably think abstractly about certain math theorems.

How quickly can your preteen add and subtract under pressure? Just gather a half dozen friends around the table for a *Hearts* game and let her be the scorekeeper for the noisy gang!

Not all of our family games involve purchased equipment. Hundreds of situations arise every year that are conducive to mental math games, and even with my "math retardation," I can be resourceful. On the way to the post office, for example, I casually mention that I have ten dollars to spend. "How many 29-cent stamps can we buy for that amount?" I ask in the car.

In the grocery store, we linger over fresh mushrooms. "Let's say I want to buy a pound today. Which is the better buy — two 8-ounce packages for $1.39 each, or one pound from the bulk section for $1.95 a pound?"

At dinner time, one child asks how old George Bush is. We get the almanac, find the birth date, and have a 20-second subtraction lesson.

As a result of playing so many kinds of games, our boys are gradually acquiring two valuable skills that should serve them well in the future:

1. They are learning the importance of reading directions. When we play a new game, we insist that they read (or listen to) the directions. If they wish to improvise later, fine. But the habit of reading directions is one that will save them considerable time and money in a thousand endeavors throughout life. It might also be the difference

between earning "A's" or "F's" on math exams.

2. They are becoming more creative and more resourceful with their leisure time. Television is no longer the magnet it once was, because beating your brother at *Chinese Checkers* is so much more satisfying than bickering with him about which channel to watch. Once they played *Sorry* with twice as many wooden tokens as the rules suggest. Another time they made structures out of old playing cards on the carpet and demolished them with a dented ping pong ball. Indoors or outdoors, our children seem to be among the first to shout, "Let's play a game!"

The rewards of gamesmanship go far beyond better math skills. We recently took a 3,000 mile car trip in December. After we arrived home, some of my friends thought I was stretching the truth when I told them that despite having totalled our car in four lanes of icy interstate traffic, we'd had a good trip and the boys had been excellent travellers. I didn't stretch anything, except maybe my pride in how our kids behaved on the road. Maybe children who play the old fashioned board games at home can amuse themselves a little longer in confined spaces. On that same trip, we checked into modest motel rooms in rural America on two consecutive nights (including New Year's Eve) with temperatures near zero, with no swimming pool, and with no shopping available. We allowed the kids to complain for ten minutes before turning off the television and unpacking the decks of cards for rowdy games of *Crazy Eights* and *Hearts*.

I'm thankful that our children enjoy playing games, both the physical ones and the mental ones. They know they're having fun, but I know that they're also learning some practical math skills, behaving (most of the time) like civilized competitors, and finding new challenges for their keen and curious minds.

From the March-April, 1993 issue of *Home Education Magazine*.

Math the Easy Way

Shari Henry

I still hate math. At least the copy-the-problem-from-the-blackboard kind. When it came time to seriously consider how I would pass on an anxiety-free mastery of the subject to my kids, I looked at all my options, carefully observing other homeschooling families along the way. Immediately, I noticed two things: there was potential to spend a great deal of money on math products such as Cuisenaire rods, DIME and pattern blocks, wrap-ups, and fraction wheels, and even the most committed unschooler relied heavily on math workbooks. Clearly, homeschoolers didn't feel math could be learned as naturally as reading, writing, science, or history.

Well, I'm all for manipulatives, and, in a way, I'm all for workbooks. Manipulatives engage children and workbooks provide a checkpoint for those of us wanting to be sure our kids learn a certain body of mathematical knowledge. But I've watched friends rely solely on math products, spending considerable time and money using them. I remain unconvinced that their method is any more effective than our ad hoc, learn-math-from-the-world-around-us variety. Required annual tests provide a vehicle for comparison, results of which allow me to claim this with certainty: Both of my children work math problems 2 to 3 years beyond their conventionally schooled peers, and equally well to any homeschooler we know.

Tim and I sit comfortably on the fence between unschooling and good old-fashioned one-room schoolhouse learning. We maintain strong opinions about the kind of education our children should have, and feel it's our responsibility (and within our authority) to pass that on to them. However, we've noticed the vast majority of information, including math, can be taught by actively living life together with our kids, occasionally filling gaps with activities that are fun, or at least, brief.

So, yes, we use our share of manipulatives, from tapes and index cards teaching skip counting to Cuisenaire rods to United States currency and coins. We use Miquon workbooks (planning to move into Saxon next year) and Math-It, and enjoy the Brown Paper School Books and anything by Anno. Both planned activities and workbooks, like vitamins, supplement our otherwise healthy math diet, sometimes providing unnecessary but added assurance, other times, fundamental nutrients we might have missed. Transferring skip counting into multiplication tables or a conceptual of addition and subtraction into writing a mathematical sentence with symbols such as +, -, and =, seems easier, to me, with a workbook.

To put this in perspective, our "school" math takes about 10 to 15 minutes, 3 to 5 days per week. That's it. Given my kids' competence levels in the subject, they're either unusually gifted (I don't think so), I'm a great teacher (Not!), the schools make way too big a deal out of teaching math and still don't do it well (okay, okay, we all know the answer to this one), or kids really can learn most basic mathematics from everyday experiences.

At first, I spent a lot of time racking my brain to find everyday ways to help build math skills. Sure enough, focusing on the major components of our lives, such as life skills (cooking, cleaning, building, paying bills, etc.), sports, recreational play, and traveling, we've been able to give both TJ and Bek strong foundations in math. As importantly, because they don't see math as a meaningless, abstract subject, separate from the rest of their lives, they lack fear and apprehension when approaching it. With a little ingenuity and a lot of patience (Bekah can take a long time to fill a plastic bag with oranges), anyone can do the same.

Shopping, cooking, cleaning, and other daily chores offer a multitude of math lessons. On a typical grocery trip, Bekah counts and weighs the produce, TJ looks for the best deals on anything from juice on a shelf to fish at the counter, and we all add up the cost together. If I see a misleading come-on, such as a big block of cheese being marked with a bright orange sticker, "ONLY $2.49 a pound, I make a point of asking the kids to grab a smaller package to compare - often the smaller ones cost less. If the kids have money they want to spend, I remind them to remember tax, and send them off to search the aisles for treats.

Cooking offers a clear stage for adding, doubling, fractions, learning about properties of various temperatures, and on and on. My kids are always allowed (and sometimes required) to help with meal preparation. Somehow, we've whittled our measuring spoon supply to only a 1/2 t. and 1 T., requiring aptitude to figure out proper amounts for recipes. Dividing up chicken equitably into individual pot pies or cutting a pan of brownies for a pot-luck requires experimentation and skill before getting it right. As the kids grow, so will their ability to help with grocery shopping and recipe deciphering, continuing to stretch their mathematical minds.

Working on the cars, building shelves and birdhouses, and renovating bicycles are Tim's domain. The kids eagerly jump in, measuring wood, counting quarts of oil, or digging through the toolbox for suitable wrenches and screwdrivers. Like grocery shopping, frequent trips to the hardware store give them the chance to help find the best deals and get a feel for costs.

The most controversial decision we've made (not to us but most of our family has voiced loud disapproval) is to include the kids in our budgeting process. If they ask why they can't have something, we rarely answer, "No, because we don't have the money," which only prods Bekah to demand, "Well, let's stop by the cash machine, then." To reasonable requests, we might answer, "We only have $450.00 (or whatever) left to go until payday and we need to pay the vet bill, buy groceries and gas, and Bekah needs a new pair of shoes." Or, to unreasonable requests, "No way, you're crazy" or "Wait 'til your birthday." I sit at the kitchen table and pay bills in full sight. TJ has begun to hang out with me, and I show him the ledger of incoming and outgoing funds. We've never hesitated to tell him daddy's salary or the amount I make writing. Both children are privy to the items on our "Most Wanted" list and the reasons for the order - root canals and crowns because they're necessary, a Kitchen-Aid mixer because it will pay for itself in a year, a computer to make mom more efficient and provide kids with entertaining educational options, and a new van before our faithful but weary Caravan needs to be led to an open field and shot. Both kids are aware of the costs of such items, how we're saving for them, and how long we anticipate saving to take. TJ managed to finagle a promised Nintendo by a car salesman if we purchase our new van from him. If I know TJ, he'll hold the guy to his word.

Aside from math skills, the kids see firsthand that cash is always better than credit, immediate gratification isn't all it's cracked up to be, and a savings account is necessary. They also see why we purchase particular things at particular times, causing less jealousy and resentment. The children have their own accounts as well. They fill out deposit and withdrawal slips and add amounts to their passbooks. They sometimes receive money as gifts, but more often have worked hard to earn it. We've set up, for them, percentage guidelines of how much they can spend, how much goes into short and long term savings, and how much they will give to charity or church. Bekah's still a little quick to spend her available share, but through the years, TJ has grown fond of putting his money away, realizing that the toys he died for 2 years ago aren't even around anymore. Also, they clearly see how God faithfully blesses their gifts to others, always multiplying what they've given, making them much less fearful about giving money away.

Some arenas take no encouragement or set-up whatsoever. TJ is absorbing swimming and baseball like a new sponge swelling with its first dunk in the sink. If a short course workout is based on 25 yards and long course on 50 meters, then his mind has to do the switching over to how many lengths of the pool he'll swim for 100 breaststroke, 200 IM, or 400 freestyle. He calculates his times over and again in various events, seeing how much he needs to shave to qualify for tougher meets. Lately, he's checking the qualifying times for the older kids, seeing where he'd be as a 9-10, 13-14, or Senior swimmer. Also, he has new respect for tenths and hundredths of seconds. We laugh at how fast that time flies by out of the pool.

And, baseball, baseball, baseball. Cards are everywhere, marks on all the walls. It'd drive me crazy, but, again, kids can't be this engrossed in anything without learning. Between calculating batting averages, timing pitches, and purchasing, comparing values, and trading cards, TJ's learned decimal points, percentages, monetary values, addition, subtraction, and division.

Even in non-organized sports, the kids and I can't get away from math. We count for hide-n-seek and hot potato (sometimes we declare a "Skip Count" game, counting by 2's, 3's, 4's or 5's), add by 2's or 3's for basketball, and figure distance in golf. Bowling and tennis are even trickier.

As we try to keep the TV off on days too cold to get out much, we play quiet games, all of which require scorekeeping. *Go Fish* and *War* introduce dividing, counting, and matching numbers, and *Monopoly* teaches addition, subtraction, percentages, and relative value.

Travel's gifts to our math classes are too generous to measure - almost. Like all bored journeyers, we guess upcoming mileage signs, subtract to figure how far we've gone (often double or triple digits), and plan for future stops using a map and a clock.

"It's 4:15, where will we be around 6:00?"

"No, we don't want to eat mid-swamp in Louisiana. How far to the next town?"

You get the picture. We use the atlas, measure different routes before and during trips, add up mileage, calculate speed limits, factor in new construction, and take our best shots, which usually end up the worst possible choices. Because we explain our limited travel budget, the kids are less likely to beg for treats at every gas or potty stop.

Admittedly, partly because I have the attention span of an ant, I couldn't imagine sitting at a table for 3 or 4 hours a day attempting to captivate my children's minds. So, it remains much more natural for me to clean, cook, shop, pay bills, and recreate together, capitalizing on the educational benefits of life in general. Our techniques and the children's involvement will evolve as they grow. When it comes to advanced algebra, geometry, and calculus, I'm sure we'll rely heavier on textbooks. But, by then, I'm equally certain they'll have solid footings on which to secure those walls, keeping the building process manageable. And, at the very least, TJ, Bek, and Phoebe will easily be able to run households, balance checkbooks, keep scores, and take trips. Sure beats spending 12 years sitting on hard chairs under bright lights, robotically copying problems from a textbook, all to be able to do much, much less in the end.

From the July-August, 1994 issue of *Home Education Magazine*.

Unschooling Math

Sue Smith Heavenrich

The principal from the local elementary school told me he had a bunch of old math texts that were being discarded — would I like to sort through them? I eagerly pawed through the pile, and managed to find a handful of first-grade workbooks missing only the first seventy pages or so. I was less thrilled a couple months later when my son tossed his book onto the floor and informed me, "This is boring." How was I going to do math?

About science, reading, music, art I never worried. I figured we'd read, something would catch our interest, and we'd get involved in projects. But I was never a math wizard. I still count on my fingers — when my children aren't looking. So I worried. As my son mentally tallied our *Uno* scores, I fretted about teaching sums. He partitioned scarce resources (chocolate chip cookies) amongst a group of friends, giving to each an equal share, and I worried about fractions.

It wasn't till we were driving home one day that I realized how needless my homeschool-math anxieties had been. "Mom," says he, "how far is it from our house to Ithaca?"

"About 25 miles," I answer.

Some silence. Then, "Wow, we'll have gone 50 miles today. How much gas will we use?"

"We burn up about one gallon for every 20 miles," I answer (My car is not politically correct).

"How much does a gallon of gas cost?"

I give him the latest figures from our local station, "A dollar twenty." I drive on, the silence deepening as he tries to figure half of $1.20.

A couple miles down the road I figure he's given up on the problem and has gone back to reading his Lego catalog. "Hey, mom, that's three dollars. How much air pollution do you think we made today?" The rest of the way home we talk about car-pooling, air pollution, alternative fuels, and solar-powered vehicles. When we get home I take a good look at his math workbook. He's right. It is boring.

I've tried to be more relaxed about "doing math", using it as a problem-solving tool rather than memorizing "math facts". We play lots of games, and use manipulatives to introduce and reinforce concepts. I try to connect numbers and mathematical thinking with other things we're doing: science, music, art, social studies. By capitalizing on my children's interests and activities, I try to draw our math lessons from their lives. We tend to do the same sorts of problems that are in the workbook, but our problems are more complex, more real. And thus, more interesting. Rather than adding 23 + 5, my son wants to add 1,235 + 250. Instead of learning to tell time to the nearest quarter of an hour, he wants to be able to calculate how long until his favorite radio show comes on the air.

For the moment, the flash cards and workbook are gathering dust, but I haven't abandoned the idea of a math curriculum totally. There are some things I think need to be learned, mathematical tools, formulas, ways of viewing problems that will come in handy later in life. As in allowing children to learn to read at their own pace, I'm beginning to understand the need to allow them to learn to think and reason in their own time. The New York State elementary math curriculum focuses on six areas: working with numbers, working with fractions, measuring, collecting and analyzing data, geometry, and problem-solving. You do some of each every year, and add complexity. Makes sense. But curriculum guides often approach topics year-by-year, so it's hard to get the overall picture of where you're going. For example, classifying and sorting is emphasized for pre-school and kindergarten, but some children are ready for more. So I went through our state curriculum outlines and reorganized it by area.

Working with Numbers

Math for young children includes sorting and classifying things, estimating, the concept of equality, counting (up to 20 or so), and some adding and subtracting. They do a lot of this informally... comparing their stash of Halloween candy with their friends, sorting through a bucket of hardware looking for nuts, bolts, and wood screws.

By second grade children are often counting to 1,000 or more, adding and subtracting two- and three-digit numbers, and beginning to use multiplication. Third and fourth grade usually introduce decimals, multiplication tables (up to 12 x 12), long division, counting by 3's, 5's, etc., and using other number systems like Roman numerals. Fifth and sixth grade math usually introduces positive and negative numbers, exponents and scientific notation, sets and subsets, as well as more sophisticated problem-solving.

There's a lot of "working with numbers" in everyday life: keeping scores for games, budgeting allowance, doing dot-to-dots, comparison shopping. Often, if I don't interfere, my children will discover concepts on their own. One day Coulter was playing with the balance, just moving the 5g and 10g masses from pan to pan. He was trying to see if he could balance the scale with different combinations of weights, and was excited to discover that 10+10+10+5 = 5+5+5+10+10.

Counting has evolved into a useful tool. I often use it as a way to measure distance while walking, riding bikes, or driving. For a five minute drive from the doctor's office to the library, I challenge my children to count to 300. In addition to helping them learn to estimate time and speed, it eliminates the nagging questions, "When will we get there?" I really do like having a couple of math workbooks around — for me to use. I like to see the range and complexity of problems normally assigned to that age, and the workbooks are great for travelling.

Working with Fractions

My husband used to teach math. One day a student walked into the classroom, took one look at the board and turned abruptly. "Fractions... I hate fractions!" he cried as he ran out the door. Why is it that when something we do every day is formalized it becomes difficult? Fractions are an integral part of everyday life around our house. If cookies are for dessert, the children need to figure out what their equal share is. Using the language of math helps reinforce the ideas of dividing things into halves, fourths, or whatever. By the second and third grade ratios are introduced, and also the concept of equivalence (1/2 = 5/10). Fractions can be related to multiplication and division in a formal way. Fourth, fifth, and sixth graders begin working with factoring, finding common denominators, dealing with proportion and scale, and percent.

One thing about fractions — once the children understand the concept, they will use it. One day I gave each boy a dozen marshmallows and a word puzzle. Something simple like: divide the total into two equal groups, now divide each half into two equal groups, etc. Then I had them eat two marshmallows and do the same thing with the remaining ten. I was looking for whole numbers, but forgot that marshmallows are soft enough to tear in half!

Measuring

Measuring things rates high on my children's list of "things to do". Tape measures, yard sticks, scales, and stopwatches are all within easy reach. After one shopping trip we left a box of canned goods on the kitchen floor. Toby was then a toddler, and at the age when rolling cans across the floor is great fun. But on this day he was more interested in measuring the tops with a tape measure, and lining them up in size-groups.

Often we'll come across a measurement in our reading. Once it was the length of a Viking longhouse, and we went outside to measure off 80 feet. We have measured the height and weight of everyone in the house, compared mud-puddle depths, and calculated the speed of travel for caterpillars.

Formal study of measurement begins in kindergarten, and continues through the grades, adding more each year. Things to measure: length, distance, mass, volume, area, time, and temperature. We use both metric and English.

Collecting and Analyzing Data

Collecting data can be as simple as using tally marks and making simple bar graphs to compare your information. In second and third grade the concepts of chance events and probability are introduced, and data collecting is more organized. In fourth, fifth, and sixth grades data is organized into charts, graphs, and tables. Children begin to look at statistics: mean, range, and sampling, probability, and independent events. You can get into unbiased sampling techniques, and do great studies on how to "lie" with statistics - how "averages" may not give an accurate picture of reality.

One of our long-term science projects is keeping track of birds at our feeders. If we graph our data, we can use our bird counts to compare populations over time, or compare relative populations of different species. As part of a water quality study we needed to know the average depth of a small river we were sampling. Coulter, who had measured the depth at 3-foot intervals, knew that it varied from 1 foot to a bit over 6 feet. We drew a picture of depth variation, a "map" of the bottom of the river, then calculated the average depth. He felt that mean depth, 4.25 feet, gave no real idea of the complexity of the river's bottom.

Geometry

There are mornings when bowls of cereal sit on the table getting soggy because my children are figuring out tangram puzzles, or making designs on the geoboards. Or they will spend half an hour creating intricate designs with colored wooden mosaic tiles, while upstairs I cut and lay out quilt pieces on the floor. Somewhere I have activity cards and notes on how to integrate these "math tools" into our curriculum... but we're so busy playing that we don't have time to read the instructions.

Usually around third grade math books introduce plane figures, compass and protractor, and coordinates on a grid. Fourth graders are busy with area, volume, perimeter, circumference, and formulas. Also pattern symmetry and mirror games. Scale and ratio are introduced later.

Problem Solving

We love mazes and strategy games. We found an old "dungeons and dragons" type adventure/quest computer game that involves exploring a maze. (Unlike modern games, the "hero" is just a cursor, and "enemies" are shown by letter.) I buy maze books by the dozen, and everyone has a chess set except me!

And we have no lack of problems. Last year the children wanted to grow pumpkins and peas in their tiny 3' x 5' garden. Their solution was to plant the peas first, and allow the vines to grow up a pole tipi. The pumpkin vines were allowed to sprawl over the rest of the bed, and the lawn, and the... Solving the problem required thinking about space and time, measuring, and using knowledge about plant growth habits that would allow a novel solution. There was only one small oversight - they couldn't reach the peas when they were ripe!

From the July-August, 1994 issue of *Home Education Magazine*.

HISTORY/ GEOGRAPHY/

Part Three - Subjects One Two Three

SOCIAL STUDIES

World History, or Starting From the Beginning

Connie Pfeil

We have been homeschooling for six years or so now. At the beginning we were with a public school independent study program, so we
tried to do social studies the way the schools did. That is to say, from
the child outward.

You know, child in the family, child in the school, child in the
neighborhood, child in the town, child in the state, child in the
nation, etc. Well, it didn't work.

First of all, "child in the school" is unnecessary for homeschoolers.
"Child in the family" starts at birth and "in the neighborhood" and
"in the town" follow as seen from the baby backpack.

So our family started with "child in the state," otherwise known as
California History, in 4th grade. We had a great time with our study
of Native Americans in this area. There are usually terrific exhibits
about Indians in state parks and we have a few around here with
reconstructed villages and people who will show you how to make the
various objects used by the native peoples.

However, when we reached the time of the invasion of the Spanish
in our studies, my daughter could not condone what the
Conquistadors had done to the Indians, nor understand why they had
come at all. (And meanwhile, what was happening on the East Coast?)

Therefore, we dropped the whole method and decided to start history at the beginning. As the native peoples of most of the world have
very similar cultural objects and objectives (basketry, pottery, hunting,
gathering, etc.), it was not hard to generalize our studies. One of the
most exciting things about the so-called "primitive" cultures is that the
children in those cultures would usually learn much of what was needed for survival by the time they were about nine or ten years old. Sure,
they needed practice, but they could help with the gathering and
bring home all they could carry, and they could hunt small animals for
the dinner pot. They would have a firm sense of their own competency and importance to the family just at the time in their lives when
they needed it.

Our "modern-day" kids need to feel this sense of competency at the
same ages, so now is a good time to teach skills like cooking, fire making, shelter building, camping skills, clothing making skills (spinning,

sewing, leatherwork, etc.). These can be learned while playing at being primitive hunters and gatherers.

From there we went on to the "first civilizations." How writing began was a good introduction to learning to read. We made a special field trip to the UC-Berkeley archeology museum to look at Babylonian and Egyptian artifacts and went to the Rosicrucian Museum in San Jose. We tried our hand at making clay figurines like those made by the Babylonians and cooked a meal using the foodstuffs available in Ur. We looked at pictures of the pyramids. We moved on to Crete and Greece and so forth.

Our method is for me to read aloud about the civilization, to look at pictures, to discuss the people and to try to imagine ourselves living in that culture. We compare the one we are currently studying with the ones we have finished. We try to cook like the people, to play games like they would have played, to make something in the manner they would have made it. We are now integrating music and art into our studies.

Every so often we leave the continuum of European history and take a "trip" around the world to see what is happening elsewhere in the same time period. We used the Usborne Publishing Company's history books as well as many books from the library, including the Time/Life Timeline books for adults. *When All the World was Rome* is a useful book for the study of the Roman Republic and Empire.

I've discovered that the more hands-on stuff I can work in, the more the cultures "stick." The more we can relate what we are studying to things that are happening today, either on the news or in our personal lives, the more the study of history makes sense — and only sensible things stay in our minds.

We still haven't gotten to the Spanish in America. We are still studying the Vikings and the rise of feudalism. But we are gaining a valuable sense of the unity and diversity of human experience, which will make it easier to see the conquest of America from Spanish eyes.

From the November-December, 1990 issue of *Home Education Magazine*.

History at Brook Farm Books

Donn Reed

Yesterday, we played the cassette tape of an old radio program called "The Battle Hymn of the Republic," the moving story of Julia Ward Howe's writing the words to go with the then-popular tune of "John Brown's Body." This morning we started another tape — "Listen to the People," by Stephen Vincent Benet. We didn't get past the introduction. (We'll try again tomorrow.)

"That name seems familiar," one of the kids said. "Don't we have a book by him?"

I stopped the tape, waiting, while the kids searched their memories and each others' faces. Finally I prompted them: "It was mentioned briefly in the tape we heard yesterday. That is, something of the same name. It's a long poem; book-length."

"Hiawatha?" asked one.

"What was the song in the story?" I asked.

"Battle Hymn —? Of the Republic!"

"Right. Where did the tune come from?"

"Someone wrote it." (Always a wise guy.)

"Who?"

"Stephen Vincent Benet?"

"Longfellow?"

"John Brown?"

"John Brown's body?"

"Right again. No one knows who wrote the tune; perhaps it just grew, as people repeated the song. Who was John Brown? Did people really sing about his body?"

And so on. Sometimes the kids know the answers, and we jog their memories. We help them gather their bits and pieces of miscellaneous information and tie them together — to relate the facts to other facts, to the world, and to themselves. Sometimes it's new to them, and we talk about our own ideas, opinions, and experiences; books we've read, places we've seen. We bring out maps, posters, more books. This morning, "John Brown" led to State's Rights, the Constitution, the Declaration of Independence, the Gettysburg Address, the Magna Carta, the Mayflower Compact, the Fugitive Slave Act, the Mexican War, the Boston Tea Party, Thoreau, slavery, Uncle Tom's Cabin, democracy, Socrates, and several usages of the word "yankee." The discussion was lively, with several puns, jokes, and lots of new understanding.

We like history. We don't like most history books. They are dull and boring, and littered with wars — not big wars, fought for principle, good against evil, but petty wars, fought for greed, money, power. Little attention is given to great thinkers, inventions, works of art, music, philosophy, medicine.

I was released from high school at the expected time, so I suppose I must have known the answers to at least half the questions asked by history teachers, such as, Who fought the Battle of Hasty Pudding? How did anteaters affect the outcome? Why was this battle important to the development of the fur trade in colonial Chicago? I have long since forgotten the answers, and I doubt that remembering them would contribute very greatly to my worth as a person or to my happiness.

We use history books, but seldom as intended by the authors. We skip and bounce, skim and dive, reading aloud, discussing what we find. We show the kids how to search out the highlights. We look for truly significant happenings in the development of humanity and society. We look for "human interest" — unusual or humorous facts which demonstrate that the people of the past were real people, like us, not just shadows or silhouettes, who ate, slept, loved, feared, and hoped just as we do. We use maps - regional, national, and the world — and a globe. We point, we let our fingers do the walking over continents, over centuries —

Some scientists say humanity began here... Biblical scholars say it began here... Here is where agriculture is believed to have started... Here, glaciers swept the continent... How did people survive?... Here was the first man to proclaim that there is only one God... Here, a new thought in philosophy, government, science, medicine, or architecture...

We look for forerunners of democracy. We trace the evolution of human government — family patriarches or matriarches, tribal chiefs, religious leaders, monarchy, oligarchy. We discuss "good" kings and "bad" kings — what made them so, and what influence did they have on society's growth? We often brush over the names and usually settle for an approximate time, such as "about a thousand years ago." For our purposes, it often makes no difference if an event occurred in 1169 or 1269. As the gap narrows, as the event is closer to us in time, a finer distinction becomes desirable. Many facts of history stand by themselves; they have significance regardless of the time in which they occurred. Other facts seem meaningless until they are put into perspective by relating them to their own time, their own place, their own circumstances. Taking the history of mankind as a whole, very few individual names, dates, or happenings have any great significance. There is no reason to memorize any of them just for the sake of "knowing" them.

We feel it's important to have an understanding of the broad sweep of history — the long journey people have made from the caves and swamps to the moon. We believe it's important to know that we of today are not the first real people; that a hundred years ago, a thousand, ten thousand, people got dressed and ate breakfast and worked for a living and taught their children; they laughed and cried; when a boy of ancient Rome skinned his knee, it hurt and bled just as it would today. We are not so greatly removed from our ancestors as we often think. Despite today's great advantages (and some disadvantages) in technology, industry, medicine, we have changed very little over the centuries. That which makes us human — whether it's the size of our brain, the opposable thumb, or a share of divinity — is unchanged.

We marvel at the scientific discoveries and advances of the last hundred years. Why did mankind crawl for so long, and then suddenly walk, run, and fly? We marvel at our humanity, our self-healing bodies, our hopes and fears. The men who have walked on the moon have the same flesh as did the students of Socrates. As we draw our fingers over the globe or map, and scan the centuries with our talk and our hands, we can back off into space for a broad overview or zoom in closely for a detailed picture. This big ball has been spinning through space for a long time, warmed and lighted by one of the dimmest stars... Down here a woman is preparing breakfast for her family. Is it charred mammoth, or corn flakes and toast? Here is a man digging a hole. A pitfall for a tiger? A hiding place for pirate's treasure? A city sewage line?

Men and women have always been concerned with good and bad, right and wrong. They have always strived for truth, for a good life, for good government. Most of the best ideas in today's governments had their roots in very ancient times. Our social growth hasn't kept pace with our technological growth (or so it often seems), but we are still advancing, moving from various forms of tyranny toward total emancipation. A very few, here and there, such as the Hopi Indians of Arizona and the Society of Friends, are models of what all humanity may one day achieve. Democracy, as visualized by the writers of the U. S. Constitution, and by Lincoln — "government of the people, by the people, and for the people" — is the highest form of government yet achieved by any large society; but it's just a stepping stone. Majority rule is better than dictatorship, but the majority is not always right, and the minority may still be misused and wronged. We wait — and strive — for the next development.

The Hopis and the Friends decide by consensus and agreement. Each member seeks what is right and good for all members; not only what is desirable for the majority, or for those with the most influence. There is no lobbying or filibustering or voting; only calm considera- tion and discussion until unanimity of opinion is reached.

"But that would take too long," some will object. "People can never agree that much. Nothing would ever get done."

That's true, of course. As most of us are now, the best we can hope for is democracy. A thousand years ago, democracy was considered an impractical dream (when it was considered at all). A thousand years from now — who knows? Our descendents will be living then, and we like to think that their society's conscience and spirit will have begun to catch up to the computers and spaceships. We hope the study of our yesterdays will help them have better tomorrows.

From the Novembe, 1984 issue of *Home Education Magazine.*

How 29¢ Can Buy The World as Your Textbook

Craig Conley

A postage stamp can be your child's passport to the world. And you won't even have to look up overseas rates. Nations establish embassies, consulates, and tourism offices in foreign countries to promote better relations between governments, and the United States is home to hundreds of such offices. Once you understand the nature of each of these offices, you can use them. They're waiting to hear from you... that's what they're there for!

Embassies

An embassy is an ambassador's office, and each country maintains only one embassy in the United States. Ambassadors deal with diplomatic relations. The Yugoslavian ambassador, for example, says, "I represent my country." His office is busy with such things as economic and commercial affairs and issuing visas for entry into Yugoslavia.

But there would be no diplomatic relations without the general public. Embassies want to spread the word about their countries. Therefore, they offer free information to anyone interested. The Yugoslavian embassy (like its counterparts from other countries) has information on agriculture, art, business, economics, entertainment, history, law, music, nature, politics, science, sports, technical data, travel... you name it.

The Yugoslavian embassy also provides a newsletter, as do most others. Ask for brochures and pamphlets, including *Facts about Yugoslavia* and *Yugoslav Survey.*

Consulates

A consulate is the office of a consul. Most countries maintain consulates in the United States. They are scattered all over, and most major cities have at least a few.

It's the consul's job to promote trade with the foreign government and to protect the rights of citizens from his country. The Icelandic consul, for example, tries to look out for the well-being of the Icelandic citizens who might live in the area.

The consul's duties don't end there. The Korean consulate says its purpose is "to promote an understanding of Korea and its culture for the American people, for the mutual benefit of both Korea and the U. S., through an exchange of personnel, trade, and culture." Accordingly, it offers such publications as *Facts About Korea* and *Korean Newsletter*.

Tourism Offices

A tourism commission is established with one aim in mind: to promote a country as a potential vacation destination.

The Kenyan tourist office, for example, provides travel information to the general public. Free publications include *People of Kenya*, *Wildlife of Kenya*, *Culture of Kenya*, and *Tourism in Kenya*.

The Australian tourist commission offers *Australia—Your Travel Planner*, which lists the country's visitor attractions and facilities, transportation, entertainment, bargain travel plans, and a wide range of practical information for vacationers.

Finding Addresses

To see if your city has a foreign consulate, check the Yellow Pages under "Consulates and other Foreign Government Representatives."

Bantam Books publishes the *National Directory of Addresses and Telephone Numbers*, which features all the information you'll need to contact foreign offices.

The Department of State Office of Media Services can assist you in finding addresses; their number is 202-632-1394.

The Government Printing Office also has information about foreign countries. Write to them at N. Capitol and H Streets, N.W., Washington, D.C. 20401.

Your library probably has the *Washington Information Directory*, published by *Congressional Quarterly*.

Making Contact

When your child contacts any of these offices, remember that courtesy counts. Most of the representatives prefer written requests.

Remember that English probably isn't their native language, and it's easier to translate a request that's in writing.

After a formal salutation, your child should briefly indicate that he is a student interested in learning more about the country. Next he should describe the type of information he desires. It's best not to request too much at one time—have your child narrow his interests to two or three main topics. Finally, your child should thank the official in advance for his time, and say that he appreciates this effort toward cultural understanding.

Allow a substantial time for the reply, as the office could potentially have to forward the request to its home country (though this is unlikely).

"Its a Small World After All"

When your child makes direct, personal contact with a foreign representative, he'll gain an invaluable perspective on the world. Suddenly, international relations are literally at his fingertips. He can actively participate in cultural exchange.

Imagine your mailman delivering the first package. Think of it as a thread helping to unite the global community. And when it comes down to it, getting mail is its own reward.

From the January-February, 1992 issue of *Home Education Magazine*.

Social Studies

Sue Smith Heavenrich

Before the first Vikings set foot upon North American soil, the United States was multi-cultural. There were more than a hundred Native American tribes, each with its own language, religion, and customs. Beginning with the earliest colonists and continuing with each new wave of immigrants, our country's population has become ever more diverse. Appreciation of this potpourri of color and culture has seldom been emphasized in the public school curriculum. Until recently. Suddenly everyone from teacher to publisher is eager to snatch up novels, short stories, and non-fiction featuring protagonists from different ethnic backgrounds. "Multicultural" is no longer just an educational buzzword; it's required reading for the '90's.

Included in the New York State Regents goals for elementary and secondary school students is the requirement for multicultural learning. "Each student will develop the ability to understand and respect people of different race; sex; ability; cultural heritage; national origin; religion; and political, economic, and social background, and their values, beliefs, and attitudes." (From *A New Compact for Learning: Improving Public Elementary, Middle, and Secondary Education Results in the 1990's*, published by the State Education Department, Albany, NY, 1991.) The intent is admirable, though in reality it sounds like trying to legislate morals.

Multicultural learning does not wait for a particular lesson plan that fits within a well-mapped curriculum. Like reading, learning to appreciate and respect the differences in others begins at home. Within the family. Like reading, it can begin simply, with reading books aloud and sharing delight in the stories and illustrations. What toddler can resist Helen Oxenbury's oversize board books that couple nursery rhymes with pictures of children of all colors tumbling about? And what pre-schooler can resist the rich detail in Patricia Polacco's picture books?

Children's literature goes beyond talking bunnies and alphabet books. Often the stories deal with difficult issues like overcoming fears, conflict resolution, or maintaining friendships in spite of differences. and an ever growing number focus on the complex interactions between children (and adults) of different cultural backgrounds. But

multicultural stories demand more than simply painting a few different faces here and there. They should include interaction between two
or more cultures, and lead to an understanding and respect for the differences. An important thing to keep in mind is that not all cultures
view the same event in the same way.

Parents (and teachers) seeking good multicultural literature may
want to keep the following criteria in mind:

- Does the author tell a good story?
- Is the story accurate (especially if historically based)?
- Does the story reflect the values of the people and the times about
which it is written?
- Is the dialogue realistic?
- Are the characters believable?
- Does the story help us understand problems of today by examin-
ing those of the past?

According to Kermit Ackley, social studies teacher at the Estee
Middle School in Gloversdale, New York, one problem with schools
is how teachers interrupt children who are reading so the class can get
on with school work. Usually this means mimeographed worksheets
designed to direct attention to the "important part" of the reading.
One of his seventh graders remarked, "I'm sure he (the author) didn't
have these worksheets in mind when he wrote the story!" I know that
if I tried to interrupt my son's reading to discuss how Prince John's
cruel taxation of the English peasants led to the Magna Carta, he'd
glare at me and retreat to his room to finish *Robin Hood* in peace. Not
everything can, or should, be discussed during the reading of a book.
Indeed, some of our best discussions come weeks later, after we've had
time to digest the stories and put them into historical perspective.

Reading stories about, and from, different cultures may enable our
children to glean wisdom they will not accept from us (after all, we're
their parents!). James Holley, director of the library in Vestal, New
York, is a pipe carrier of the Sioux people. In the past, elders played an
important role in Indian life. Maybe we need to re-include them within our own society, he suggests. We need to have respect for the peoples and their teachings. He has a point. Perhaps in learning about the
old ways we can discover solutions to the dilemmas confronting us
today.

Aside from the richness and diversity found in books, there is
another reason to integrate children's literature in our studies. We can
use well-crafted stories to model the kind of writing we want our chil-

dren to do. Textbooks do have their place... they are full of factual material, great for research. But, forsooth!; you cannot get a feeling for the language unless you dive into real books with real stories. No textbook would describe the beloved grandmotherly woman in Patrica Polacco's *Chicken Sunday* as having a voice "that sounds like slow thunder and sweet rain."

Incorporating Literature Into Your Curriculum

One of the advantages of home education is that learning is not divided into separate subjects. Things blend. Reading about the Revolutionary War might lead a child to investigate biographies. Those stories may, in turn, bring up questions that touch on the environment, agriculture, or technology, as well as the social milieu.

If one wants to emphasize the interconnectedness between people, environment, and events, trade books are an excellent resource. Often a good book can become a jump-off point for study. Novels and biographies come immediately to mind, but don't overlook diaries, poetry, and nonfiction. Books about the ecology of a region or technology and inventions add insight and understanding. There are many ways of incorporating literature into your homeschooling curriculum:

- Use a theme for a frame of reference, and select a variety of books that fit.
- Focus on a region, perhaps the Sierras or tropical rainforests.
- Choose a time period and collect books from, and about, that time.
- Check with your local library. Often they have lists of books relating to particular topics.

From the January-February, 1994 issue of *Home Education Magazine*.

OTHER STUDIES

Part Three - Subjects One Two Three

Nobody's Perfect

Daine Chodan

Often, enrichment for a home educated child deals with the child's strengths. Music lessons for the child who has shown ability, accelerated programs in reading or math, or expert coaching for the athletically gifted child come to mind. These types of activities obviously make sense, and of course we should continue to provide these opportunities.   However, it interests me how much benefit my child has received from extra lessons dealing with her relative weakness. Anneke is not a gifted athelete, yet she takes horseback riding and swimming lessons. I purposely chose individual sports that could be enjoyed without a team. One obvious benefit derived from working on these activities is a growing physical ability and confidence. My daughter works to perfect her own technique rather than to "beat" some other child. Yet it will be possible, if she chooses, to join a swim team independent from a school team.

Unexpected (and maybe more important) benefits have emerged in the form of some interesting attitudes Anneke expresses. My daughter now understands that not everything comes easily. What a wonderful antidote to the "if I can't get it right away forget it" attitude fostered by her incredible quickness in reading and math.

She has learned the value of continued effort. It took her four series of classes before she passed the Red Cross Beginner's level in swimming. While she was disappointed the times she did not pass, her teacher, her father, and I were able to point out the areas of improvement on her progress card. Each time she took lessons, she finished more requirements. She recently received her swimmer's card, a real accomplishment for any nine-year-old, but nevertheless a tough six-year battle for my child. It is interesting to note that many adults and children seeing her in a non-class situation feel she is an exceptionally good swimmer for her age. They did not see her class in which she was most often the last swimmer to finish her laps.

Anneke can empathize with slower children. I have never seen her laugh at a child having problems doing something. She will say something like, "John must feel sad about reading. It's like the time I tried and tried to learn that crawl stroke." She is also exceptionally able to pick out the gifts in others. She may say that one of her friends has trouble in math but draws very well.

Anneke can enjoy an activity even if she is not best at it. She genuinely likes to swim and ride. Recently, she asked to take a series of ice skating lessons. She eagerly anticipated the classes even though she couldn't skate as well as many of the other children. She discussed what she did learn and pointed out that she fell fewer times each class. She is less intimidated by difficulty.

Most importantly, she understands that we recognize her wonderful abilities, but we don't expect her always to be best. By supporting and encouraging her in activities like these, we are telling her she doesn't have to be perfect.

From the June, 1987 issue of *Home Education Magazine.*

Music to their Ears

Craig Conley

My mom taught a course in music appreciation when I was growing up, and I didn't even know that I was her student or that our living room was the classroom. Any parent can instill in his child an appreciation for all types of music, and most of the "instruments" are probably already in your home.

Can "Appreciation" Be Taught?

Music has some unusual properties which can make it seem difficult to understand. Unlike paintings, which you can examine closely for a long time, or sculpture, which you can study from all sides and even touch, music is an art form that is fleeting. It's here one moment and gone the next. It invisibly fills the room, and yet takes up no space. It surrounds you and even starts working inside you—perhaps making you feel happy enough to start dancing, or perhaps making you feel serious and sit quietly—and yet you cannot touch it. Music is certainly magical, but it need not be mysterious.

Your child doesn't have to know anything about music to know what he likes and what moves him. But the more he does know, the deeper his enjoyment becomes. He may or may not like any one type of music, but if he has an understanding of it then he will appreciate it.

The unique nature of music doesn't mean that listening to it has to be a passive experience. Your child will like music passively, with his ears, but he will learn to appreciate and love it actively, with his eyes and hands. And you can get him started with the following concrete techniques.

Begin with Something Familiar

Start by playing some music that you already have in the house—anything will do—and have your child draw pictures. The more natural the environment, the better. I remember the day my mom put on Alvin and the Chipmunks' *What's New Pussycat?* album for us to listen to. My brother and I drew anything we wanted, but most of our pictures turned out to be in some way inspired by the song that was playing at the time (though no one told us to do that). We did this every day for a week or so, always to a different record, but with no guidance whatsoever.

Then one day mom brought out a roll of paper and suggested that we try drawing a "road map" of the sound: one continuous line that twisted and turned to the music. We ended up with a sort of diagram or transcription of the music, which looked very much like a map. After we finished, mom played the same music again so we could "read along," following the music as it danced down our squiggly line.

The Only "Required" Music You'll Need

Our reward for doing all of our lessons one day was Prokofiev's *Peter and the Wolf* (you can find this at most record stores, or try a college media center or learning resource library). This is a symphonic fairy tale which is narrated and "illustrated" by solo orchestral instruments. Each instrument represents a character or a sound effect in the story, and children learn to identify the instruments by their sounds. It's very entertaining to listen to, but your children will probably enjoy drawing pictures to accompany the story. By now they are learning to actively visualize images to go along with music. This is an important skill for shaping one's own interpretation of a particular piece.

The Historical Angle

To fully appreciate music, however, your child must have a feel for how and why a particular piece developed the way it did. One natural way to introduce this idea is to find an appropriate picture book in the library (try the oversized shelves). Most album covers provide enough background information on the artist and time period for you to determine a suitable companion. My mom found David Macaulay's book *Cathedral* for me, and when I sat down to look at it she put on some choral church music (I think it was by Mozart). She didn't have to tell me that such music was played in a cathedral—I instinctively knew it because it fit the pictures in the book perfectly. Later she found a book of photographs of Vienna, Austria, and played some Johann Strauss waltzes when we looked at it together. The pictures came to life with the rhythm of that music. Similarly, a collection of paintings of New Orleans' French Quarter was the perfect match for an album of Dixieland jazz music. Such picture books provided me with an important historical perspective. I was learning where broad types of music sit in relation to world happenings and situations.

Individualized Projects

Reading: The picture books whetted my appetite for more information. There are a number of excellent biographies of famous musicians written for children. I loved the series titled *Childhood of Famous Americans*, which includes the stories of such composers as John Phillip Sousa and Stephen Foster. I always listened to music by the composer in question while I read about him. The more I found out about the people who wrote music, the more fascinating their music became. For instance, when I discovered that Beethoven spent his last twenty years partially and then totally deaf, I couldn't wait to listen to music that he composed in those years. I had a whole new reverence for it, and would sit for hours marvelling how he could hear that music only in his imagination. I made a game of trying to recall certain passages of his music in my head.

Writing: Mom encouraged me to write in stream-of-consciousness style about how a particular piece made me feel, and speculate about what a particular composer was trying to "say" through music. I was actually required to do the very same exercise later in a college writing class, so I was well prepared.

Live Performances: Our town didn't have its own symphony, but my family always went to concerts when groups visited. Later, when we moved to a bigger city, I volunteered as an usher at the local orchestra. I handed out programs to people as they approached their seats, and then got to stay and listen to the concert for free. At most universities, every music class performs at the end of the semester, and most of these concerts are free and open to the public. You will probably discover some unusual groups. Two particularly interesting performances my family attended were by a Percussion Ensemble (instruments which usually don't get much notice) and a Marimba Ensemble (an instrument we were totally unfamiliar with. It's similar to a xylophone.).

They're All Ears

You don't have to know how to play an instrument or have studied the history of music to spark your children's interest. Merely providing some background music will put them half-way down the road to being musically literate. Before you know it, folk, symphony, opera, jazz, rock, bluegrass, vocal—all will be "music to their ears."

From the November-December, 1990 issue of *Home Education Magazine*.

Your Own Arts & Crafts Group

Kate Raymond

Betsy, my five-year-old, and I are extroverts and thrive on social contact. Before we committed ourselves to homeschooling, we wanted to know if there were other local homeschoolers who might like to play with us on a fairly regular basis. Since my daughter, her younger brother and I all enjoy art projects, we thought an arts-and-crafts playgroup would be the perfect way to meet people.

The actual start-up of the group was simple. We placed a small announcement in the local homeschool newsletter asking if there was anyone else interested in meeting once a week to do arts and crafts. I did not place any age limits, but did mention the ages of my children as a way of focussing the group's activity level.

We received four calls in the next two weeks and were able to set up a mutually agreeable time for our first meeting at a nearby park. On that first of many Mondays to come, our group, which eventually grew to five moms and fourteen kids, fell into a pattern that felt very natural. We would generally arrive at the park anywhere between 10 and 10:30 am, and whoever was there first saved a table while the kids played. Waiting was never a problem with the swings nearby.

Once everyone had arrived we set up the art supplies and let the kids go at it. As you'd expect, project times varied, ranging from 20 minutes for painting paper plate mobiles to about an hour and a half for sewing designs on burlap. Our group usually met for one and a half to two hours.

We were also flexible about the flowing back and forth between the playground and the art table. The young boys in our group seemed to spend twice as much time playing with each other as creating art, which was fine with us. Letting them find their own level of involvement was the whole point, right?

The arts and crafts group was everything we had hoped for. My children made new friends who were homeschoolers. Important, I think, when almost everyone else they knew was going to public school. We also got to see how other families do the nuts and bolts of homeschooling, and we got some great new ideas for art projects.

It's surprising to me that over the past two years we rarely did the same thing twice. We've made bread dough art, finger paintings, Ojo de Dios, clay sculptures, origami, bead necklaces, Fruit Loop necklaces (a big hit), kites, spin art, chalk drawings, hand puppets and face painting, not to mention seasonal crafts like our candy decorated gingerbread houses last Christmas.

Besides getting craft ideas, I also greatly benefitted from hearing other parents' ideas about education. It was during this time that I grew to appreciate the advantages of not preparing art projects in advance as models for the kids. One of the other moms advised me to let them create whatever they wanted, no matter how far away their finished projects were from my ideal.

I also had support in unlearning the ways I thought education had to take place. Through words and example, my arts and crafts friends showed me that I could relax. My children would learn when they were ready to, not when I thought they should.

Because I felt more relaxed and determined not to nag or suggest, my daughter was able to continue painting her "every inch covered with tempera" paint specialties until she decided it was time to try some rainbows and stick figures. And without my help, she has now moved on to drawing people with necks. My son also is very happy dabbing and blobbing away, and I feel no need to help him develop his technique. (Okay, occasionally I do have twinges!)

But throughout it all, the most marvelous thing is that they are both enjoying themselves, enjoying the act of creating.

An incident occurred about five months ago that really drove home the lesson I learned on the benefits of keeping my hands off my children's creations. A neighbor asked me to watch her five-year-old daughter on our arts and crafts morning, so we brought her along with us. That morning, I think we were making collages — something very free-form. I remember looking around at all of us busy with drawing, cutting, and gluing and then seeing this little girl just sitting, staring at her blank paper.

I asked if she was all right, if she needed something. She answered that she didn't know what to draw, that she didn't know how to draw anything. We tried to help her get some ideas, but she finally ended up copying someone else's drawing and then tearing it up in disgust when "it didn't turn out as good as hers!" I'm not sure why she was having so much trouble, but my guess is that she has rarely encountered a blank paper without having a lot of directions to go along with it. She had never learned to trust her own creativity.

That incident renewed my resolve to stand back as much as possible, to let my children find and trust their own ideas. They are having fun discovering and learning. It's the best gift I can give them.

Recently our gathering have come to a temporary end. One family is moving to Oregon, another family is not yet back from a long vacation, others have found new interests or have summer plans that make regular schedules too binding. We are glad to have a break to work on projects at home.

Our arts and crafts group has served its purpose. Our family has found our niche in homeschooling. In the fall, maybe we'll reorganize and put the word out that a new arts and crafts group is starting — or possibly a science and arts group? Who knows? We're creating!

Tips on Starting an Arts & Crafts Group

• Put an announcement in your local homeschool newsletter and/or the local newspaper.

• If ages are important to you, mention in your ad that you have younger or older children, so you will have a core group of that particular age. It's not difficult to adjust projects for younger or older siblings.

• When people respond to your ad gather the following information: days and times when they can meet, ages of children, expectations about the kinds of arts and crafts you will do, expectations about whether or not parents will be expected to attend.

• For the first day, you may decide to bring the art supplies or someone else may volunteer. This is a good time to brainstorm a list of future art projects and decide if you'll take turns bringing supplies, contribute funds towards art supplies, or just all bring what you have at home. We mostly followed the latter approach.

• Take time to introduce yourselves to each other and warmly welcome any late-comers. You may also like to exchange phone numbers and talk about what happens when a family can't come. Our group members almost always called someone else in the group if they weren't able to come, and absent members had the responsibility for finding out what the project was for the following week.

• Before you leave that first get-together decide what the project is for the next week.

• After your group has jelled you may want to discuss if you are open to new members and if everyone needs to agree before a new family is invited. Our group was very informal, and we just invited anyone who was interested. Most of the time this worked fine, but I think if we do this again we may want to set up a loose procedure. Probably, we should at least mention to the other members that we are thinking of inviting someone else unless there are any objections.

• Eventually the weather will get cold and it will be time to move inside. If your group is large, you may want to break it up into more manageable smaller groups and meet at different houses, or you may be lucky and have the use of a recreation room or church hall, etc.

From the September-October, 1993 issue of *Home Education Magazine.*

Special Education for Homeschoolers

Robert Staten

Public Law 94-142, the Education for the Handicapped Act, requires that every disabled student in America receive a "free appropriate public education." However, many school districts take the view that providing services within their buildings satisfies that responsibility. If parents choose to withdraw from the system, their children need not be served. But in fact, the law does not define a particular setting in which Special Education must take place. If your child has a disability which prevents him or her from benefiting from traditional instruction, even traditional home-school instruction, there is probably a way to access Special Education services.

Probably the most formidable obstacle standing between you and Special Education is the complexity of the system. To reach your goal, you will have to work through a bewildering maze of regulations and standards that seem agonizingly restrictive and redundant. Even though you know your child better than anyone else possibly could, don't expect to beat down the system with your powers of persuasion alone, or even common sense. The legal requirements represent a long struggle on the part of parents to protect their handicapped children, and every regulation is intended to safeguard them in light of a history of public abuse. As far as the federal government is concerned, the hoops are there to guarantee the rights of children, and you will have to jump through them along with everyone else. So you might as well know the rules.

The first step is to identify your child's handicapping condition. Most such conditions fall into one of four categories; physical handicaps (blindness, deafness, or impairments such as paralysis) mental handicaps (retardation), learning disabilities (including speech and language disorders, attention deficit disorders, and sometimes autism), and behavioral/emotional disorders. Within these broad categories, each state is free to develop their own specific definitions, and to describe under what conditions students will qualify for services because of them.

The definitions vary widely from state to state. In New Mexico, where I teach, the State has recently incorporated exclusionary clauses into its definitions. These clauses state that the above mentioned conditions may not be the result of economic or experiential deprivation or lack of fluency in the English language. In addition, the handicap must actively interfere with a child's ability to learn in order to be a qualifying factor.

Still, the law charges each state with identifying handicapped students wherever they are. Federal funding can be withheld from a state which is proven not to be actively involved in this process. So, most States will evaluate a child who is referred by his or her parents, even if they do not attend public school.

To initiate a parent referral, contact your local public school district administration's Special Education department by phone, and let them know your concerns. Be prepared to document why you feel your child needs Special Education, and what strategies you have used to alleviate the problem. Strategies typically cited by public school teachers include preferential seating, individual tutoring, specially designed lesson plans, and opportunities to work at the student's own pace. Since these are precisely the kinds of things that take place in your homeschooling environment, they should be included in your referral report. Some states require more formal screening, but samples of your child's work and detailed descriptions of your homeschooling activities should be taken into consideration as well.

Once a student is evaluated, the school district must convene a meeting to determine whether he or she is eligible for services. You, as a parent, must be advised of this meeting and reasonable arrangements made to allow you to attend. You can bring whoever (and as many) people with you as you need to support your case. At this meeting, your child's testing will be reviewed to see whether the scores fall into any of the above mentioned eligibility categories. If you have anecdotal records that complement or contradict the district's test results, be sure to bring them with you.

Once your child's eligibility is established, the next step is to plan an appropriate educational program for him or her. In Special Education this is called an Individual Education Plan, and it is the legal document that dictates what measures outside of regular education must be provided to a student. There is nothing in the law which prevents the writing of an IEP containing elements of both public and home-school education, but such a plan will be highly unusual in the experience of the district employees with whom you are dealing.

This is where you are likely to encounter a second major obstacle. The laws governing Special Education are complex and open to interpretation. At the school level, teachers and Principals may not be aware of recent trends, or policies. I taught Special Education for fifteen years, more than half of them as head teacher for my department, and it was only in the course of doing research for this article that I discovered my district has a policy of advising parents of homeschoolers about special services whether they ask or not. My experience had been that when parents of handicapped children withdrew them from school, we put their folders away in a drawer and waited.

Once having established your child's eligibility and identified his or her needs, the debate will focus on how to provide the necessary support.

Obstacle three. Money. When the IEP is finally signed, that document encumbers the district to provide whatever services are outlined therein, so if there is a less expensive option to providing service at home, your district will undoubtedly prefer it. This is the point at which negotiations are most likely to break down.

If this happens, there are three approaches you can take. The first is cooperation. You can always schedule additional IEP meetings to develop whatever plan you feel is most appropriate for your child. Thoughtful discussions may result in some compromise that all parties can live with. This could include a combination of homeschooling and Special Education at a district site, having public materials and resources made available to you, or home visits from an itinerant therapist. If you don't get satisfaction at this level, you may have to escalate your approach to a more confrontational one. As the parent of a handicapped child, you have a lot of power. Once having established your child's eligibility, and failed to develop an IEP with district representatives, you can initiate an appeal process, called arbitration, which may ultimately result in a negotiated agreement. Once again, the intent of the law is to ensure you and your child maximum access to necessary resources. If you go to arbitration a couple of important factors work in your favor. First, the arbitrator must be an outside party upon whom you and the district both agree. More importantly, however, the district must abide by the decision of the arbitrator, but not you.

The third and final stage is litigation. This is the most extreme, expensive, and time-consuming approach to achieving your goal. However, sometimes it is necessary to carry the fight all the way to court in order to meet your child's needs. Courts are very sympathetic to the cause of handicapped children, and tend to rule in favor of parents more times than not. Favorable rulings have required school districts to provide disputed services, reimburse parents who have paid for private services, and even pay court costs and legal fees in some cases.

There is a danger in this approach, however. In your search for services, you will already have found that school administrations are willing to do almost anything, if it does not tax their already heavily-burdened resources. When you initiate a court action, the district spends so much money on arguing its case that they must show a favorable result in order to justify the expense. So they will probably take a hard line. This is particularly true if you are the first to apply for a service or program. You may set a precedent that others will follow, further encumbering the schools district's meager funding. Litigation should be viewed as a last resort, to be used only when all other options are exhausted.

Every child has a right to an equal share of America's educational pie. Whether they are taught in a public classroom, or at home, the law (and common morality) demands that handicapped children have access to whatever special services are needed to provide them with an equal opportunity to learn. Work with your local administrators to find the most appropriate way to satisfy those needs, and everyone will benefit.

From the July-August, 1994 issue of Home Education Magazine.

ADVANCED LEARNING

Part Four

What Do We Really Mean by Higher Education?

Helen Hegener

The term "higher education" is generally taken to mean schooling beyond the twelfth grade — college and further intellectual or vocational studies. To us, the term signifies something a little bit different. It encompasses the entire range of possibilities available to our children as they begin maturing and move toward adulthood.

These possibilities are quite different from those traditionally thought of as suitable for the group which we'll loosely define as teenagers. Largely unencumbered by the demands of structured schooling, our homeschooled kids can select their own activities for learning about the world, activities such as learning a skill or an art or a craft, holding down a part-time or full-time job, being politically or socially active, travelling, playing sports, building their own business, doing volunteer work, locating an apprenticeship or an internship in work they'd like to learn, and yes, even going on to college.

How can we support our youngsters in their explorations? In the Foreword to Britt Barker's book, *Letters Home* (Home Education Press, 1990), Britt's mother, Penny, writes, "I have never felt that I was preparing our children for anything but living and so when Britt was 18 we didn't automatically consider that it was now time for her to enter a university or other institution for some 'serious education.' Instead, Richard and I early on began to help Britt search out experiences in her areas of interest. In fact, when we see that the children have an interest in anything, we give them our help in pursuing that interest. On the other hand, the children's individual interests come after the family's breadwinning work here on the farmstead and that presents daily decision making, planning and motivational challenges."

With our own five children, now ages 7 to 18, we've always focused on the present, pointing out possibilities for future exploration whenever we could, but keeping our attention - and theirs - on what's happening here and now. We see our role as helping them to discover new ideas and to try new approaches, but also to steadily build a strong foundation of confidence in their abilities, based on practical experience with a wide variety of activities and endeavors.

Building on experience necessitates helping to provide a child with experiences. When they're toddlers we cheerfully take our children to the park so they can experience swings, slides, sandboxes, and being with other kids their own age and size. As they get older we help them select and buy musical instruments or art supplies or puppies, we drive them to lessons and parties and meetings, and we plan endless outings to museums, art openings, music festivals, and other events which will add to their supply of experiences. But as our children grow older, and start doing much of this planning and providing for themselves, we might rightfully wonder how we can best help them now. Tradition holds that once a child moves in the direction of self-sufficiency we parents should back off and let the fledgeling fly away.

Nancy Wallace, author of *Child's Work* (Holt Associates, 1990), writes about this notion of what she terms "letting go" in her chapter Moving Outward, "Another idea that we tend to think about in the abstract, instead of as connected to a meaningful purpose, is the idea of 'letting go.' As a mother, this has been one of the most difficult and frustrating notions I've had to deal with. We are continually advised to 'let our children go,' as if 'letting go' makes perfect sense - as if it's possible and even desirable for children to 'go,' without having any reason to 'go' or any specific place to go."

This is a question parents have wrestled with from day one, but an ever-increasing dependency on experts and institutions has only undermined the natural abilities of mothers and fathers when it comes to recognizing what their older children need (and don't need). Childhood experts tell us that we shouldn't be "overprotective" of our children. Magazine articles warn of the "stifling effects" of not allowing our children to do what "all the other kids" are doing. And we fall prey to these uncertainties. Nancy quotes a delightful passage from Jean Leidloff's *The Continuum Concept*: "Ever more frequently, our innate sense of what is best for us is short-circuited by suspicion while the intellect, which has never known much about our real needs, decides what to do."

Agnes Leistico writes in her book, *I Learn Better by Teaching Myself* (Home Education Press, 1990), "We chose the educational option of homeschooling our three youngsters primarily because we want them to have a life long love of learning and to feel good about their ability to learn. We recognized that each of them had their own approach to learning. Each youngster has rewarded our faith in them to choose wisely what is of importance to them. At no time do we want to close any other educational options, though. We need to continually reassess their progress and mistakes, but we also expect to learn from these errors in judgement."

Making mistakes and learning from them. A somewhat novel approach in today's guideline-filled world. The old trial and error approach has gotten some pretty bad press recently. Now days there's a right way and a wrong way to do everything, with how-to books, newspaper advice columnists, magazine articles and video how-to's to ensure that we do it with a minimum of fuss and bother. And some of the most popular and pervasive how-to-do-it directions concern raising our kids.

Kathleen McCurdy, who began homeschooling her five children long before most people had even heard the word, wrote about her family's approach in the May/June, 1989 issue of *Home Education Magazine*, "Gradually we evolved a philosophy of education: Home schooling means children apprenticing to their parents for the basic skills of life. By taking advantage of experiences that are part of daily living, by participating in normal activities at home, by being involved in their parents' activities and interests, children learn the important skills necessary for survival in our society."

This common sense approach, so simple and yet so far removed from the typical American family's experience, easily explains homeschooling's appeal. Children who spend two-thirds of their day at school are not apprenticed to anyone. They're shuttled endlessly between breakfast and the school bus and classes and recesses and lunch and classes and the school bus and after-school activities and piano or dance lessons and dinner and homework and bed. And in what most people term "higher education," this situation is magnified and intensified tenfold. At the same time that life is beginning to assume some pretty confusing proportions, most youngsters are thrown into a suffocating atmosphere of academic study and told that their future success in life rests on how well they adapt to it and perform.

Grace Llewellyn, author of the no-nonsense book, *The Teenage Liberation Handbook: How to Quit School and Get a Real Life and Education*, tackles this foolishness head-on when she writes about her discovery of the writings of John Holt: "Essentially, he argued that learning is a natural process that happens to anyone who is busy doing something real for its own sake, and that school confuses and destroys this process."

In adopting the methods and devices of schooling we perpetuate this confusion and destruction, and the natural process of learning becomes a frenzied scramble for the best curriculum and the highest test scores. And while this might make perfect sense to the parent of an eight-year-old, it somehow loses it's irrefutability when that same youngster is twelve or fourteen. A kind of parental panic starts to take over and whispers that "soon it will be too late!"

If we teach our children *how* and *why* to learn, instead of *what* and *when* to learn, we will be providing them with "important skills necessary for survival in our society." Spend an afternoon or an evening just talking with your youngster, exploring ideas and sharing opinions, discussing likes and dislikes, daydreaming and wishful thinking, and you'll both come away with an idea of what direction to nudge the learning in. Watch for opportunities to share an interest, or for the two of you to tackle learning some new skill together. The time we have with our teenagers is even more fleeting than the time we had with our toddlers, and we should strive to share as much of their lives as they want us to.

Quite a few writers have cautioned that we should help our children keep their options open. Donn Reed, author of *The Home School Source Book* (Brook Farm Books, 1991), writes, "We try to show our children the broadest fields of possibilities, always emphasizing that there's no need to make a choice; that following one's own interests and instincts, not as a goal but as an exciting journey, will lead naturally to a happy, creative life. If a child of ten or fifteen has a particular talent or interest, and is determined to follow it, that's good — provided that determination doesn't become a dutiful consistency without a continuing interest. How many adults would like to change careers or lifestyles when they're thirty or forty or fifty, but don't dare to, or don't feel capable of doing so? Any earlier choices made should allow for the possibility of a more desirable alternative suddenly popping up at any time, and the freedom of thought and circumstance to accept that alternative.

"Some public schools encourage children as young as eleven or twelve to choose their academic or vocational futures. Twice that age is a much better time for such choices, if they must be made. We encourage our kids not to make choices and decisions, but to watch and explore their own feelings and desires; to watch their general inclinations, and follow them, but without committing themselves beyond their present interests."

But what about those families who value college attendance, who dream of seeing their children in gowns and mortarboards, and whose children want to enter degree-necessitating fields such as medicine, law, engineering, or pediatrics? If the collegiate experience is important enough to them, these families will find ways for their children to meet the requirements. There are numerous examples of homeschoolers who have gone on to college without any problems, even very selective and elite colleges. These bastions of higher education (in the fullest sense of the word) value learning and inquiry, and recognize that truly motivated homeschoolers can become some of their best students. But promises of admittance to college should not become the carrot dangled enticingly in front of the student. Likewise, homeschooling efforts should not be judged on the outcome, or the product.

In their book *Homeschooling for Excellence* (Warner Books, 1988), David and Micki Colfax wrote, "As the late John Holt correctly observed when Grant's admission to Harvard was gaining widespread publicity, a homeschooling program should not be considered a success or failure on the basis of whether or not a child is admitted to an elite college. Homeschooling programs have, and should have, different objectives, derived from the interests and needs of the children and parents. Our program reflected, in what one homeschooler called it's 'practical bookishness,' our academic and ranch experiences, and well served our boys when it came time to apply to colleges. Had we been homeschoolers who had been, say, boat builders, musicians, or artists, it would have been different in at least some respects — and almost certainly less college-preparatory. Perhaps Grant would have by now become a master boat builder, Drew a sophomore at Juilliard, and Reed a sculptor."

Higher education could probably be defined as what happens to us for most of our lives. Once we've learned the basics, the readin', writin', and 'rithmetic, we spend the rest of our days adding to our stores of knowledge in a million different ways. There are very few things we do in our daily lives which don't in some way add to our knowledge and affect how and why we do things.

In the final chapter of *Teach Your Own* (Delacorte, 1981) John Holt wrote, "What makes people smart, curious, alert, observant, competent, confident, resourceful, persistent — in the broadest and best sense, intelligent — is not having access to more and more learning places, resources, and specialists, but being able in their lives to do a wide variety of interesting things that matter, things that challenge their ingenuity, skill, and judgement, and that make an obvious difference in their lives and the lives of people around them."

From the November-December, 1992 issue of *Home Education Magazine.*

Homeschooling the Older Child

Mary McCarthy

I've noticed that I run into more supposedly mature people who have no recollection whatsoever of having been 15 years old. They have no memory of having done dumb 15-year-old things or having an acute case of "awkward teenage blues". They do not remember when their feet were too big, the boys too short, the girls too tall, or their nose any of the above. They have forgotten about that time in their life when everybody else got to do all the things their parents wouldn't let them do. Given this, parents who choose to educate their own teenagers at home are special people — and with luck, they will have a special insight into this very strange time of life.

Adolescence is the age of trial and error. It's trying on being an adult while not quite ready to give up being a child. The results can be anything from tragic to hilarious. It's difficult not to laugh when a child who is taller than you stomps through the house crying "You won't let me grow up!" While you or I can see the humor, the adolescent is very serious and expects to be taken that way. They believe that they are perfect and parents are the root of all evil. (Remember?)

All teenagers, like all grownups, are different, and what works with one may not work with another. But there are basic ideas which apply. The first is to recognize that this person is an individual and due the respect you would give any other individual. It's important that their individual interests be acknowledged and they be involved in their own educational decisions. Ask them what they want to learn and why. Negotiation plays an important role. It is fair to both parent and child to let each select a course. For example, the child who has no other ambition in life than to play the drums in a rock group should be encouraged to play drums AND to study math — so they will be able to manage all those millions of dollars they will make.

It's important to remember that this is a "hands-on" age. By the time they are teens, just reading about the Civil War will not be equalled by one day of running around Gettysburg.

What about the adolescent who is removed from the public school system to be educated at home? One of the most important things stressed in public education is the social life which is supposed to prepare these young people for adulthood.

In *The Third Wave* Alvin Toffler writes about the "covert curriculum" of the public education system. He explains that it is made up of three courses: "one in punctuality, one in obedience, and one in rote repetitive work". The first thing your adolescent needs is time: time when they don't have to learn, to follow rules, be on time, or produce on demand. It's a big adjustment.

This naturally curious age needs to redevelop that stifled curiosity and rediscover learning without the judgement of peers. Don't be surprised if it takes a year before the confidence returns. Encourage each seemingly little success - each leads to increased self-confidence and bigger successes. Eventually, you'll be rewarded every time you bit your tongue when it seemed that your kid couldn't do anything but stare at reruns of "Charlie's Angels". The growing self-confidence, pride and sense of achievement will make it all worthwhile. Promise.

Finding curriculum materials requires a little more imagination than with elementary ages, but there's also more flexibility. With a higher reading level more of the world is opened up for use. And the increased ability to absorb information makes the educational value of museums and "tourist attractions" double that of the younger children.

Sometimes it helps to just throw "education" out the window and just get to know this interesting person. Go to the beach! Play video games! Enjoy this wonderful age of discovery! And if, perchance, you *do* remember the good times of being a teenager — here's your chance to enjoy them all over again!

From the October, 1986 issue of *Home Education Magazine.*

Houses, Boats, Families, and the Business of Schooling

John Taylor Gatto

I want to give you a yardstick, a gold standard, by which to measure good schooling. The Shelter Institute of Bath, Maine will teach you how to build a three thousand-square-foot, multi-level Cape Cod home in three weeks' time, whatever your age. If you stay another week, it will show you how to make your own posts and beams; you'll actually cut them out and set them up. You'll learn wiring, plumbing, insulation, the works. Twenty thousand people have learned how to build a house there for about the cost of one month's tuition in public school. (Call Patsy Hennon at 207-442-7938 and she'll get you started on building your own home.) For just about the same money you can walk down the street in Bath to the Apprentice Shop at the Maine Maritime Museum and sign on for a one-year course (no vacations, forty hours a week) in traditional wooden boat building. The whole tuition is eight hundred dollars, but there's a catch. They won't accept you as a student until you volunteer for two weeks, so they can get to know you and you can judge what it is you're getting into. Now you've invested thirteen months and fifteen hundred dollars and you have a house and a boat. What else would you like to know how to do? How to grow food, make clothes, repair a car, build furniture, sing? Those of you with a historical imagination will recognize Thomas Jefferson's prayer for schooling—that it would teach useful knowledge. Some places do: the best schooling in the United States today is coming out of museums, libraries, and private institutions. If anyone wants to school your kids, hold them to the standard of the Shelter Institute and you'll do fine.

As long as we're questioning public schooling, we should question where there really is an abstraction called "the public" at all, except in the ominous calculations of social engineers. As a boy from the banks of the Monongahela River in western Pennsylvania, I find the term insulting, a cartoon of social reality. If an institution that robs people of their right to self-determination can call itself "public;" if being "public" means it can turn families into agents of the state, making parents spy on and harass their sons and daughters because a schoolteacher tells them to; if the state can steal your home because you can't pay its "public" school taxes, and courts can break up your family if you refuse to allow the state to tell your children what to think—then the word public is a label for garbage and for people who allow themselves to be treated like slaves.

A few weeks is all that the Shelter Institute asks for to give you a beautiful Cape Cod home; a few months is all Maine Maritime asks for to teach you boat building and rope making, lobstering and sail making, fishing and naval architecture. We have too much schooling, not too little. Hong Kong, with its short school year, whips Japan in every scientific or mathematical competition. Israel, with its long school year, can't keep up with Flemish Belgium, which has the shortest school year in the world.

Somebody's been lying to you. Sweden, a rich, healthy, and beautiful country, with a spectacular reputation for quality in everything, won't allow children to enter school before they're seven years old. The total length of Swedish schooling is nine years, not twelve, after which the average Swede runs circles around the over-schooled American. Why don't you know these things? To whose advantage is it that you don't?

When students enroll in a Swedish school, the authorities ask three questions: (1) Why do you want to go to this school? (2) What do you want to gain from the experience? (3) What are you interested in?

And they listen to the answers.

Can you build a house or a boat? Can you grow food, make clothing, dig a well, sing a song (your own song, that is), make your children happy, weave a whole life from the everyday world around you? No, you say, you can't? Then listen to me—you have no business with my kid.

In my own life, with my own children, I'm sorry I lacked the courage to say what Hester Prynne, the wearer of the scarlet letter, said to the Puritan elders when they tried to take away her daughter. Alone and friendless, dirt poor, ringed about by enemies, she said, "Over my dead body." A few weeks ago a young woman called me from Stroudsburg, Pennsylvania to tell me the state had just insisted she stop homeschooling her little girl, Chrissie. The state was going to force her to send Chrissie to school. She said she was going to fight, first with the law, although she didn't know where the money would come from, and then by any means she had. If I had to bet on this young, single mother or the State of Pennsylvania to win, I'd bet on the lady because what I really was hearing her say was "Over my dead body." I wish I'd been able to say that when the state came to take my own children. I didn't. But if I'm born again I promise you that's what I will say.

A few days ago I got a call from a newspaper that wanted some advice for parents about how to launch their children into school. All the reporter wanted was a sound byte from a former New York State Teacher of the Year. What I said was this:

Don't cooperate with your children's school unless the school has come to you in person to work out a meeting of the minds—on your turf, not theirs. Only a desperado would blindly trust his children to a collection of untested strangers and hope for the best. Parents and school personnel are just plain natural adversaries. One group is trying to make a living; the other is trying to make a work of art called a family. If you allow yourself to be co-opted by flattery, seduced with worthless payoffs such as special classes or programs, intimidated by Alice in Wonderland titles and degrees, you will become the enemy within, the extension of state schooling into your own home. Shame on you if you allow that. Your job is to educate, the schoolteacher's is to school; you work for love, the teacher for money. The interests are radically different, one is an individual thing, the other a collective. You can make your own son or daughter one of a kind if you have the time and will to do so; school can only make them part of a hive, a herd, or an anthill.

Museums and institutes of useful knowledge travel a different road than schools. Consider the difference between librarians and school-teachers. Librarians are custodians of real books and real readers; schoolteachers are custodians of schoolbooks and indentured readers. Somewhere in the difference is the Rosetta Stone that reveals how education is one thing, schooling another.

Begin with the setting and social arrangement of a library. The ones I've visited all over the country invariably are comfortable and quiet, places where you can read rather than just pretend to read. How important this silence is. Schools are never silent.

People of all ages work side-by-side in libraries, not just a pack of age-segregated kids. For some reason, libraries are neither age-segregated nor do they presume to segregate readers by questionable tests of reading ability. Just as the people who decoded the secrets of farming or of the forests and oceans were not segregated by age or test scores, the library seems to have intuited that common human judgement is adequate to most learning decisions.

The librarian doesn't tell me what to read, doesn't tell me the sequence of reading I have to follow, doesn't grade my reading. Librarians act as if they trust their customers. The librarian lets me ask my own questions and helps me when I need help, not when the library decides I need it. If I feel like reading in the same place all day long, that seems to be okay with the library. It doesn't tell me to stop reading at regular intervals by ringing a bell in my ear. The library keeps its nose out of my home, too. It doesn't send letters to my mother reporting on my library behavior; it doesn't make recommendations or issue orders on how I should use my time outside of the library.

The library doesn't have a tracking system. Everyone is mixed together there, and no private files exist detailing my past victories and defeats as a patron. If the books I want are available, I get them by requesting them—even if that deprives some reader more gifted, who comes a minute later. The library doesn't presume to determine which of us is more qualified to read that book; it doesn't play favorites. It is a very class-blind, talent-blind place, appropriately reflecting our historic political ideals in a way that puts schools to shame.

The public library isn't into public humiliation the way schools seem to be. It never posts ranked lists of good and bad readers for all to see. Presumably it considers good reading its own reward, not requiring additional accolades, and has resisted the temptation to hold up good reading as a moral goad to bad readers. One of the strangest differences between libraries and schools, in New York City at least, is that you almost never see a kid behaving badly or waving a gun there—even though bad kids have exactly the same access to libraries as good kids do. Bad kids seem to respect libraries, a curious phenomenon which may well be an unconscious response to the automatic respect libraries bestow blindly on everyone. Even people who don't like to read like libraries from time to time; in fact, they are such generally wonderful places I wonder why we haven't made them compulsory—and all alike, of course, too.

Here's another angle to consider: The library never makes predictions about my immediate future based on my past reading habits, nor does it hint that my days will be happier if I read Shakespeare than if I read Barbara Cartland. The library tolerates eccentric reading habits because it realizes that free men and women are often very eccentric.

And finally, the library has real books, not schoolbooks. Its volumes are not written by collective pens or picked by politically-correct screening committees. Real books conform only to the private curriculum of each writer, not to the invisible curriculum of some German collective agenda. The one exception to this is children's books—but no sensible child ever reads those things, so damage from them is minimal.

Real books are deeply subversive of collectivization. They are the best known way to escape herd behavior, because they are vehicles transporting the reader into deep caverns of absolute solitude where nobody else can visit. No two people ever read the same great book. Real books disgust the totalitarian mind because they generate uncontrollable mental growth—and it cannot be monitored!

Television has entered the classroom because it is a collective mechanism and, as such, superior to textbooks; similarly, slides, audio tapes, group games, and so on meet the need to collectivize, which is a central purpose of mass schooling. This is the famous "socialization" that schools do so well. Schoolbooks, on the other hand, are paper tools that reinforce school routines of close-order drill, public mythology, endless surveillance, global ranking, and constant intimidation. That's what the questions at the end of chapters are designed to do, to bring you back to a reality in which you are subordinate. Nobody really expects you to answer those questions, not even the teacher; they work their harm solely by being there. That is their genius. Schoolbooks are a crowd-control device. Only the very innocent and well schooled see any difference between good ones and bad ones; both kinds do the same work. In that respect they are much like television programming, the function of which, as a plug-in narcotic, is infinitely more powerful than any trivial differences between good programs and bad.

Real books educate, schoolbooks school, and thus libraries and library policies are a major clue to the reform of American schooling. When you take the free will and solitude out of education it becomes schooling. You can't have it both ways.

From the March-April, 1993 issue of *Home Education Magazine*.

Moving Out Into the World

Mark and Helen Hegener

Thirteen-year-old Jody asked me again the other day, "Mom, what can I do to earn some money?" And, as usual, we ran through the list of possibilities, and then thought up a few new ones — none of which were quite what she was looking for. Earning one's own money has been a recurring refrain as our children get older and seek to take some measure of control over their own lives. It's been a particular challenge because we live twenty miles from the nearest small town; there are no newspapers to deliver, no toddlers to be babysat, no dogs to walk or plants to water while the owners are on vacation — though Jody has fed our neighbor's cats while they were away a few times.

But jobs, especially those traditionally earmarked for young people, are scarce where we live. Yes, there is our family publishing business, but having been raised with it none of our kids seems particularly inclined to take it on as a steady diet. They want something a little more exciting than sitting in front of a computer...

Many homeschooling parents must be asking these same questions: how do we help our older children take that larger step into the adult world, how do we make the transition easier for them (and for us?), now that we've chosen a path away from traditional schooling with its convenient "career counselors," "vocational training," and "career preference testing?"

A few homeschooling families have experience with finding apprenticeships and mentorships, or helping their older children locate vocational or on-the-job training situations. Homeschooling families are involving their children in family businesses, or helping their children create businesses of their own. Just as these families have learned about education on their own, now they're extending that experience to learning about business and making a living. However, this is uncharted territory for most of us. We have no experience in such matters, and there are few resources for parents who want to help their youngsters find work in the world. There are serious considerations, such as how can we foster respect for traditional means of livelihood? How do we even begin to understand the tremendous diversity of jobs available in today's computer-dependent, high-tech world, much less determine whether or not these jobs are worth doing? And how do we translate that understanding into help for our teenagers?

One of the true strengths of homeschooling has always seemed to be that our children live in the day-to-day real world, and they know, from first hand observation and experience, what it takes to get along in life. They have a realistic sense of what actually happens in the "adult" world. The children of friends who attend school seem somehow distant and removed from such practical considerations.

John Taylor Gatto has spoken forcefully about what schooling does to kids by taking up all their time with abstractions. In an article for *The Sun*, Spring, 1990, titled "Why Schools Don't Educate," he wrote "In centuries past the time of a child would be occupied in real work, real charity, real adventures, and the real search for mentors who might teach what one wanted to learn. A great deal of time was spent in community pursuits, practicing affection, meeting and studying every level of the community, learning how to make a home, and dozens of other tasks necessary to becoming a whole man or woman."

With the advent of schooling, and perhaps more significantly, with the unparalleled growth and proliferation of a consumer-oriented society, this "time of a child" has been increasingly occupied with training in how to take one's place as a good little consumer, fighting the global economy wars. But who really benefits from all of this?

Many writers have examined the role of schooling as it relates to progress and development; thousands of books and articles have traced the relationship between the growth of the educational bureaucracy and the socioeconomic monolith. Now, as big business unabashedly rides in to salvage our troubled school system, it becomes more and more obvious that the emphasis in education today is on producing those all-important consumers. In *Alternatives In Education* (Home Education Press, 1992) Larry and Susan Kaseman write, "The insistence of those in power that children be raised so that they will become willing participants in the American consumer economy has led to an increasing reliance on schools to instill the necessary thoughts, beliefs, and values in children."

As homeschooling parents we've questioned the place of schooling in our families' lives, but perhaps we have not realized that questioning this societal propensity for consumerism comes with the territory. We've taken the lead in finding new ways of raising our families and helping to build our communities. Perhaps we should now help our children find new definitions of work worth doing.

From the January-February, 1993 issue of *Home Education Magazine*.

Apprenticeship for a Teen

Vivienne Edwards

The summer after we took Leonie out of seventh grade, she decided she would like some kind of work to do. Now she has always been very good at drawing and cartooning so I suggested she try to use that talent in some way. After a bit of consideration she said that she did not want to try and earn money from her hobby. She felt that the enjoyment would be lost if she was compelled to do it. So we started looking around our area for something else. As we live in a fairly rural area we thought we were going to have a problem. However, in May, when the girls went for their dental check-up, our dentist remarked that he was looking for someone to help out in the office for a few hours a week over the summer. Leonie has always been drawn towards some type of medical career and she was very interested.

She started working there in June, doing whatever hours they needed, usually 2:00 p.m. to 5:00 p.m. After a few weeks she told us that she was learning to clean rooms, bring in patients and put a movie on for them, and clean and sterilize instruments, as well as answer the phone and do office jobs like filing. Slowly she spent more time working with the dentist. She was very interested in all the procedures and he started telling her how different things were done. In the fall when it was time for her to resume her "school" work, she stayed on at the dental office, doing her "school learning" in the mornings. This usually consisted of a lot of reading. She read dental magazines, dental books loaned to her by a friend, and even books by well known brain surgeons.

At that time my husband, who is an engineer, was working on a robot controlled 3D X-ray machine for brain surgery so between them they cleared the local library of every book on brain surgery!

Also at about that time we discovered that the University of Texas had a correspondence course on Dental Assisting, which we sent for. Leonie was in seventh heaven when it came. It was a four part course, designed for a year's work. She spent every waking moment, when she was not at work, studying, and by Christmas had finished the entire course. She was 14 years old at the time.

Gradually she did more and more in the office. Of course she was not licensed by the Dental Assisting Board so she could only do certain things and had to be supervised directly by the dentist. We inquired about getting her certification and were told that she would have to attend an accredited school for one year, at the cost of about $4,500. We asked if there was another way. Yes, you can work 3500 hours and apply to challenge the exam. She decided to wait. Meanwhile she took another correspondence course, from the University of Wisconsin.

As soon as she had turned 16 (the legal age to leave school in this state) she started working full time. She could, by then, run the whole office single-handed. She did insurance claims, filed charts, and knew all the dental procedures by heart, including those for orthodontics and endodontics. Just after her 17th birthday the office manager left and then, when another office manager came, taught the job to her. Finally, last summer, she had completed her 3500 hours of work. She took the 5 hour DANB exam in Minneapolis and passed with flying colors. She was 17 years old.

I know that in doing this she has been lucky. She found a professional person willing to give her a chance to prove she could do a good job and learn what was needed as she went along. We are very proud of her and what she has accomplished, but we are sure it is no more than many other young people could accomplish, given the opportunity.

If you have a young teen who is anxious to get out into the real world, there are a number of ways to help them find what they want. You will notice I said what they want. It is no use a parent's finding "a job" and pushing the youngster into it if they are unwilling. The interest must come from them in the first place. Once you have identified the kind or kinds of things they want to do, start talking to as many people as possible in that field. Most professional people and business owners will be willing to make suggestions or even let your teen spend some time just watching or helping out in their business. Almost any kind of business will be helpful to a young person who wants a taste of "real life."

There is no need for your teenagers to be committed to a career before they go looking for work. If you live in a town, the opportunities are probably more abundant, but there should be chances for youngsters in the rural areas, too. We found that one of the best things to do is to "talk it up" everywhere you go. If your teen has a particular thing in mind, try to think of as many ways as possible for them to have contact with that career. For example, if the theater is their main interest, even offering to help clean up at the local theater is better than slinging hamburgers. They will be happier and they will almost certainly not stay doing the cleaning for long, particularly if they show enthusiasm for everything they are asked to do. One of the main complaints I hear from local business people when they employ high schooled teens is that they act dead from the neck up and have to be prodded into life before they do their job. Most homeschooled children have a very enthusiastic attitude to life, and that will go a long way towards getting them into a job they like.

True apprenticeships are very popular in England, and for that matter, in most of Europe. We are from England, and my husband did a five year apprenticeship with a large car manufacturer. The apprenticeship included college classes as well as "real work" experience. By the time he had finished his five years he also had a degree in engineering. Unfortunately this type of work/college blend is not much used in this country, although in Grace Llewellyn's excellent book, *The Teenage Liberation Handbook* (Lowry House, 1991), she mentions some apprenticeship opportunities. She does point out that many of them may be too structured for the unschooler. However, do not despair, for with some planning and perseverance you should be able to tailor a self-made program to fit your needs. We are also glad that we collected information from State Universities on their correspondence programs. We would otherwise never have known about the Dental Assisting classes. Some Universities offer very diverse and creative classes and most can be purchased for "no credit" if you wish.

If, after exhaustive searching, you cannot find an opening anywhere for your teen, don't exclude the possibility of them starting their own business. When our other daughter, Michelle (also homeschooled), came out of college at 17 with a diploma in commercial photography she could not find a job. She said her ultimate dream was to open a photography studio of her own, so with a little encouragement from us and virtually no financial backing at all she took the plunge and did it. Now, two and a half years later, her little one person studio is doing very well and if she ever needed a learning experience, that was it!

Obviously, if your teenager wants to be a surgeon, then it is not very practical to think of your own business! However, working for a local veterinarian would give them a very useful background. Even if they do end up going to the local hamburger joint, encourage them to think not in terms of being the junior but of management positions. One young homeschooled girl near here was Assistant Manager of a Dairy Queen when she was 15.

In Leonie's case, she has decided to make a career of dentistry and wants to go on to dental school. It will no doubt be hard for her to go to college after being in the work force for more than three years. However, when she started at the dental office we talked a lot about her future options, including training for a dentist. Now she thinks she would like to be an oral surgeon. We say, "Go for it!" The sky's the limit for these young entrepreneurs.

From the May-June, 1992 issue of *Home Education Magazine.*

Community Colleges

Bernard Marcus

Every year countless thousands of high school graduates attempt their first major step toward independent adulthood: they leave home for college. For many the experience is a bad one. Many seventeen and eighteen years olds are simply unprepared for the rigors of college. Reasons for this vary. They include poor preparation in high school, inadequate study skills, emotional immaturity, or simply the inability to handle the trauma of leaving home. After all, the abrupt shift from the safety of home to the real world is traumatic and some kids simply are not ready to make it by eighteen. This may be especially true for the home schooler who has not had the chance to learn to deal with a threatening environment in high school. For such youngsters, a good place to begin their college educations may be in the local community college.

In the thirty years between 1950 and 1980, the number of institutions of higher education in America increased by more than 75 percent. Almost two fifths of these were publicly funded two-year community colleges that have opened since 1960. Indeed, between 1960 and 1980, the number of community colleges nearly doubled and by 1980, approximately one third of all colleges fell into this category. They enrolled about 4.8 million, a third of all college students. This figure is expected to increase to 40% by the year 2000.

Public two-year colleges have been around since 1907, however, their numbers grew only slowly until the sixties. At that time, competition for space at conventional colleges was keen as the babyboomers and their immediate predecessors struggled for entry. Many students were denied entry; many more were unable to perform satisfactorily and failed out. It was generally believed at the time that without a college education a young person had no hope for a meaningful career.

Simultaneously, the military draft and the unpopular war in Viet Nam were breathing down the necks of more than a few eighteen year old males who were looking for some kind of refuge. It was under these circumstances that the community college became prominent in American education. Open door admissions policies made such schools available to any high school graduate, and remedial courses allowed those who were not well prepared to catch up. For a while, community colleges were popular starting places for students bound for four-year schools and universities. Indeed, there was some thought that eventually, most or all high school graduates would begin their academic careers at two-year institutions.

Times have changed. The growth of community colleges, like that of most institutions of higher education, is over. Today they compete with other colleges for a dwindling number of students. Still, the community college is a significant force in American higher education; a look at it is worthwhile, particularly if there's a chance that your son or daughter may end up at one.

By community colleges, I specifically mean publicly funded, post-secondary institutions that serve a local or regional population. They are quite apart from private, two-year junior colleges, technical institutes, or satellite campuses of universities. Generally community colleges offer a variety of career programs such as secretarial science, nursing, or police science as well as university parallel transfer programs in these and other curricula including the traditional liberal arts. In a few states, community colleges are funded fully by the state college or university system, although this is not usually the case. Most community colleges have local or regional sponsors who contribute up to one third of the operating capital. Student tuition usually accounts for another third, while state contributions make up the remainder. In some cases, local funding may make an institution vulnerable to local political whims, and in most cases, curricular offerings are influenced by local market conditions. Even so, it is difficult to characterize a typical school. Some are extremely large and well provided for. They may occupy several campuses and offer a wide variety of programs. They may have courses and equipment that compare favorably to those available to freshmen and sophomores at major universities. Others are small enough to be contained in a single building and offer only a minimum of courses and programs. In any case, a successful graduate of a community college emerges with either an associates degree or a certificate of study and then either transfers to a four-year institution to pursue a baccalaureate, regardless of what kind of curriculum he followed, or else goes looking for a job.

For a young person who is looking for a marketable skill in the shortest possible time or has a particular vocational goal in mind, a community college may well be the best place to get training. However, if your child is after a traditional college education, the choice is not so clear.

There are some aspects to community colleges that make them very attractive. For example, they are generally much more affordable than conventional colleges. In addition, students can often save room and board costs by living at home. In an age when financial aid is disappearing, these are serious considerations, and they certainly ease the trauma of breaking away from home. Additionally there are developmental and remedial courses available for students who need them. Community college faculties are usually adequately prepared. Most have earned masters degrees and a fair number are Ph.D.s. A community college instructor is likely a better teacher than his counterpart at a four-year school, but he has to be. He is probably under no obligation to carry on research nor compete for grants; therefore he is theoretically more accessible to students. A common observation by community college graduates who have transferred to four-year schools is community college professors take more of a personal interest in their students; they care.

In terms of admission, most community colleges practice what is called an "open door" policy. This means anyone who possesses high school transcripts and a diploma, including home schoolers who have worked through a local district, will be accepted. There are no competitive exams, extensive credential checks, nor interviews. Not all higher education institutions are that favorably disposed to home schoolers and other non-traditional students. All entering students generally are required to take placement exams and there is no guarantee that all will be able to enroll immediately in their chosen programs. In other words, the open door is to the institution only; admission to a particular program may first require meeting prerequisites including, perhaps, remedial work.

For the independent home schooler, the one who has not registered with a local school district, a community college door is still open, but it may be a back door. If a student does not possess a valid high school diploma, none of the colleges I checked will allow him to matriculate. However, all appear to have mechanisms available so that such a student can earn an equivalency diploma. Once he has it, he may matriculate, though again, possibly not in his chosen major. He may have to complete a series of prerequisites first.

On the negative side of the coin, a community college instructor carries a substantially heavier teaching and student load than do instructors at four-year schools. Because community college teaching is more demanding, this limits his effectiveness and makes him much more vulnerable to burnout. He may not be able to offer as complete a course as he should nor have the time for out-of-class work on student assignments. He may also be forced into adopting instructional strategies that are convenient but less effective. Furthermore, community college instructors have been criticized for expecting and demanding too little of their students. In addition, many community colleges are on limited budgets which means they may be short on state of the art equipment in some technical programs. Such schools have been accused of being "bottom-line" institutions, i.e. curricula offerings are more often dictated by expense than they are by academic considerations. Critics of community colleges have complained that, for this reason, programs are often chaotic. This also hampers teaching, and learning, effectiveness at community colleges.

Many community colleges rely heavily on part-time instructors. These may be professionals in specific areas who are sharing their experience with the students or they may be people who are teaching to supplement their incomes. Taking courses from such individuals may or may not benefit the student. There is no clear answer.

Outside of the classroom, the community college environment is not exactly an intellectual one and the typical community college student is not, to be kind, academically gifted. Indeed, he probably ended up in the lower half of his high school graduating class and failed to develop good study skills. The apparent relative freedom of college, in contrast to high school, often is misunderstood and quickly abused. Consequently, community college students habitually cut classes, fail to get assignments done on time, and frequently drop out.

Such people may make for a bad influence on a capable but not well motivated student. Consequently, even bright, young people, in such an environment, may experience academic difficulty without pressure from well motivated peers to keep them going. Alternatively, some youngsters find coursework at the community college so easy, success comes without much effort. These may experience "transfer shock" when they enter four-year schools as juniors unprepared for the work that is demanded of them.

This is not to say that community college graduates are condemned to frustration and failure. On the contrary. Many succeed enviably. Indeed, any student capable of and willing to put the required effort into his studies can take advantage of what is available at a community college and use it as a start for his higher education. It requires a fair amount of motivation and maturity to resist cutting classes and procrastinating on assignments, but, after all, the same characteristics are necessary for success at four-year schools.

In summary, community colleges have their strengths and weaknesses which each student and his parents must consider, along with financial and intellectual resources as well as ultimate goals, before deciding whether or not to attend one. And if the decision is positive, the community college provides only the opportunity for an education. It is up to the student to take advantage of it.

From the January-February, 1993 issue of *Home Education Magazine.*

How These Kids Turn Out

Earl Stevens

Sometimes people who are somewhat skeptical about home education say to me, "Well, it'll be interesting to see how these kids turn
out." In my own family, sometimes Jamie's grandmother says, "I just
hope I live long enough to see what comes of this."

I ask them all how we will know when the time arrives to judge the
result, and how will we know what to judge. Nobody seems to know
exactly. We think it has something to do with being eighteen years old
or maybe twenty-one. Will Jamie go to a good college? Will he go to
any college at all? Will he wear a jacket and tie, or will he "work with
his hands?" Will he push a supermarket carriage up and down Forest
Avenue looking for returnable bottles and muttering about his bad
luck in being born at the beginning of that cursed home education
fad? Will he wish that we had sent him to military school?

Some time ago David Colfax, with three sons accepted by Harvard
and the media gobbling it up as the epitome of home education success, wondered aloud if going to Harvard is really the most important
thing that a person can do. He had met a woman whose daughter was
working as a volunteer in the jungles of South America with a medical team combating serious diseases among Indian tribes. David
lamented that the media had little interest in this sort of thing and
would not regard her story as one of "success." Conventional wisdom
holds that Ivy League schools are about success. Innoculating Indian
children is not.

As you approach eighteen years of age you're supposed to have a
master plan. The plan can be flexible, it can even be a bit vague, but
there must be a plan. Eileen's son, Bo, turned eighteen this year.
People ask, "What are your plans for college?" Out of simple curiosity Bo and his family have driven through several college campuses
while on their way to other destinations. Bo is able to say truthfully
that he has looked at MIT, Notre Dame, Harvard, Yale, and Indiana
University. Bo says that he rarely needs to add anything to this.
Perhaps questioners worry that if they keep asking questions they'll
have to listen to a long critique on the merits of each university.

Should a person go off and do something academic or occupation-
al upon turning eighteen? Is there something about this age that is dif-

ferent from other ages such as seventeen or nineteen or twenty-one? Certainly there is nothing wrong with being an eighteen year old college student. We might expect that many of our kids will indeed follow that path. But as long as we have resisted so many other things having to do with schooling, we should support each other in resisting the notion that young adults in our families must go off and prove themselves in conventionally acceptable ways.

Last year a local newspaper ran a story about a young woman of seventeen: "A homeschool student living in Portland who hangs out at Green Mountain Coffee Roasters and Cafe No. She dresses in leotards, spiked boots, fishnet lace and lipstick—all black." There was a half page photograph of her and her friends looking like they had just stepped off the set of a Mad Max movie. Hmmm, I thought, home education advocacy groups probably won't be interested in using this to illustrate the benefits of home education.

After briefly discussing a fashion show (one with lots of chain mail) that she helped stage, and the way people stereotype her because of the way she dresses, and her hope for the future (she's pessimistic), the young woman was asked what made her happy.

"Reading. I'm a bookworm. I like Sylvia Plath, Anne Sexton, Theodore Roethke - Sylvia Plath and Anne Sexton both committed suicide - and Edna St. Vincent Millay. I've been writing for three or four years. I just basically do it because I have the need to write. And hanging out with my friends. My mother and I get along great - we have the strangest relationship. We're like best friends rather than mother and daughter. It's very beautiful."

How will this person turn out? Do we know yet? Can we ever know? Perhaps she'll write poems or go to college or help Indians in South America. Perhaps she is just a person with a life who, like all of us, must find satisfaction and meaning in her own way. Like people everywhere it is up to her to define life for herself and decide for herself what is important and what isn't.

Home education, and life, is not about doing what people expect us to do. Home education isn't about families with scrubbed cheeks, perfectly done hair, and matching outfits sitting around the kitchen table studying American history. You can do that, but it isn't a requirement. And life isn't about academic success and a career on the fast track. You can do that too, but it isn't a requirement.

Whether or not we can see or agree upon "how things turn out," perhaps the goal for each of us is real knowledge. John Gatto says,

"Real knowledge has to be earned by hard and painful thinking; it can't be generated in group discussions or group therapies but only in lonely sessions with yourself. Real knowledge has to be earned only by ceaseless questioning of yourself and others, and by the labor of independent verification; you can't buy it from a government agent, a social worker, a psychologist, a licensed specialist, or a schoolteacher."

Real knowledge frees us from institutional thinking and helps us to find meaning for ourselves instead of depending upon others to show us the way.

And what about me? How have I turned out? Am I okay? I'm sure there are differing opinions on this, depending on who you ask. My own opinion is I'm still finding my way, and I hope not to be finished any time soon.

From the November-December, 1993 issue of *Home Education Magazine*.

NETWORKING

Part Five

In Search of Community

Earl Stevens

Like many others in our culture, I grew up in an environment where it wasn't possible for children to know or even to see much of the adult world. My world was made up primarily of school, of play with other children, and of the routines of family life. Family life in my family sometimes afforded glimpses into what adults thought about and did, but most of what I saw was pretty well filtered. The nitty gritty stuff, the trials and joys and endeavors of adult life, came through to me mostly piecemeal and mostly by accident.

Adult visitors to my family spoke to me to say hello and good-bye and to say a few words about how much I had grown or to wonder politely how I was doing in school. Then the visiting adults would sit down with my parents and the mysterious curtain of adulthood would descend, separating them from me. If I attempted to linger and listen somebody was bound to wonder if there was something else I could be doing. My job was to remain reasonably inconspicuous. Children who too frequently attempted to insinuate themselves into the affairs of adults were often assigned chores to keep them busy or sent off early into getting-ready-for-bed routines.

It wasn't that the adults in my life didn't like children (although I have wondered about some of them) or that they conspired to keep me ignorant. It wasn't anything personal, it was just the way things were in our culture. Adults were adults and children were children. But the result was that by the time my friends and I were approaching adulthood we had astonishingly meager practical information and very little notion of what it meant to be an adult, far less in many respects than any twelve-year-old shepherd in Afghanistan might know about the lives of adults in his culture.

Looking back on my childhood, what I wanted most was to be recognized as a thinking person and introduced to some of the available information about living on this planet. I didn't expect or want adults to pretend that I was one of them. I just wanted to make contact, to communicate with them at a level that was above the trivia of school and the routine requirements of daily life. It was very hard to find adults who took children seriously enough to talk at any length with them. But there were exceptions, and they stand out in my childhood memory like mountains on a plain.

There was my grandmother Carrie, the inventor of hot cocoa, cinnamon toast, and kindness. What was most amazing about her is that she would sit and talk and listen to me. I don't mean she would nod in my direction occasionally while I talked and she did something else or that she would allow me a chance to prattle while she paused in the middle of lectures about neatness and civil behavior. No. She would sit down in a chair with her own cup of cocoa, look me in the eye, and we would have a long conversation. We talked about me, about her, and about the world. Best of all, she talked to me in the same way she talked to the mailman, to the farmer who lived next door, or to one of her friends who would visit for tea.

Another adult who took me seriously was Tony, a short, wiry Italian man who was a part of my grandmother's circle of friends. He wasn't talkative and openly humorous like my grandmother, but the kindness and respect ran just as deep. What I liked best about Tony was that he didn't seem to know that I was a kid. He talked to me as though I were one of his fishing buddies and knew as much as the best of them about the mysteries of finding fish. "You think there's any fish around that pile of rocks over there, or you think we should try the beach?" he would ask me on one of our trips to the Connecticut shore. "I wonder should we use sandworms or clams for bait?" This would result in a long conversation and then, after both our opinions had been duly considered, a decision. We fished all day and sometimes hardly talked at all, but I basked in my maturity and in the privilege of being with this man. And I learned to fish.

On my mother's side of the family there was a distant cousin Walter from somewhere in central Europe. He came to this country with little more than a suitcase, a young wife, and an old pistol wound received in the course of resisting the German occupation of his country during World War II. In his new country he worked very hard and became a successful dentist and a symbol for our family of the power of education. We saw that people who went to college and then into a profession made a lot more money than laborers in Hartford's typewriter factories. Walter lived a different kind of life in a large home adorned with paintings where he listened to symphonies on a giant Hi-Fi console.

But to me Walter became a symbol not of financial success but of how wonderfully different and interesting adults could be, especially when they allowed me into their lives. Walter would take me to a camp out in the country where he occasionally went to hide from a life that had become too busy. We followed animal tracks and studied the night sky. He told me stories of a time and place where it was dangerous to have an opinion and where a bag of flour or a handful of potatoes was a treasure. He never gave me advice to study hard or to respect my elders. He just talked with me, one person to another, and I learned many valuable things that I am sure neither of us would have expected.

What these people in my life had in common was that they freed me from being locked up in perpetual childhood, at least while I was with them. These were adults who revealed themselves to me and allowed me to reveal myself to them. I thought adults had learned all the rules and knew what they were doing. It was a little scary but exhilarating to find that life was more creative than that. It was astonishing to me that adults experienced hope and fear, disappointment and satisfaction, courage and insecurity Carrie taught me a lot about my worth and how to stand up for it. Tony showed me things about confidence and the quality of being quietly attentive to things outside myself. Walter taught me about how strange the world is and how peculiar and interesting it is to be alive among others. As John Holt might have said, they were early members of the faculty in my personal university.

It was a great benefit to have had these few adult friends, but I would have liked many more of them. In my adult life when I take an interest in woodworking, piano playing, or fly fishing, I keep an eye out for a person who knows how to do it. When I find a person who is competent and perhaps intelligent and agreeable, I attempt a relationship. Sometimes the person becomes a mentor, sometimes a wonderful friend as well. Right now I'm hunting for somebody who knows how to build cabinets and bookcases, something I'm getting ready to do. It would be nice if I could find an agreeable cabinet maker who also knows how to play the banjo. You never know. I have been amazed at what I find when I take the time to ask other people about their interests.

Schooling is largely responsible for the social division between adults and children because schooling defines children so relentlessly as different from the rest of the world, and it confines them in classrooms while the rest of the world is working and playing. Schooling erects a formidable barrier between children and adults. Homeschoolers have more opportunities to maintain relationships with adult friends because they have more opportunities to witness and participate in the adult workaday world. In the past year I have heard of or read about homeschooled kids working with an artist, a craftsperson, a veterinarian, an ecologist, a carpenter, a dressmaker, and a computer programmer, to name just a few instances. These aren't necessarily the careers that these children will follow, but such experiences are invaluable ways of learning what it is to work and what it is to be an adult.Homeschooled children have a unique and valuable opportunity to become integrated into community affairs and adult life at an age when most children are struggling with what we have come to recognize as an artificial, oppressive, and isolated environment. It is ironic that when school officials express public concern that homeschooled kids are not becoming socialized, the children in their care are being crowded into age segregated classrooms away from the world. John Gatto, New York City's Teacher of the Year, talked about this in his acceptance speech:

In centuries past, the time of a child and adolescent would be occupied in real work, real charity, real adventures, and the search for real mentors who might teach what one really wanted to learn. A great deal of time was spent in community pursuits, practicing affection, meeting and studying every level of the community, learning how to make a home, and dozens of other tasks necessary to becoming a whole man or woman.

I think this is much harder to do now, even for people who are very strong about these values. Gatto says, "We live in networks, not communities, and everyone I know is lonely because of that." I suspect that one of the major reasons why many of us have spent years listening to Garrison Keillor's *News from Lake Wobegon* is that we find the image of his community so compelling. In many parts of the country it is difficult to discover a community, but it is not impossible. Homeschooling is, in part, a discovery of both family and community, and homeschooled children are in a good position to search for mentors for their personal universities, to do meaningful work, to engage in charity, to have real adventures.

From the May-June, 1991 issue of *Home Education Magazine*.

Support Groups: How to Find or Start One

Barbara Hummel

Support groups can be a big benefit to homeschooling families, and they are a great way to make friends for your kids and yourself. Most people have some form of a support system, whether it's a few friends who meet once in a while at the park or a large organized group with activities and meetings, or just a friend to call when your day doesn't seem to be going very well.

During my eight years of homeschooling, I've been in three different groups, been an active, working member of all of them, and I've helped to organize the one I'm in now. I'd like to share some of the things I've learned.

What Can a Support Group Do?

A support group can provide encouragement and information for new homeschoolers.

Revitalize seasoned homeschoolers.

Provide a set of people who share similar interests, from which to make friends and gain confidence.

Provide a place for homeschooled children to meet other children (this is especially important for teens).

Become a community resource for people interested in home-schooling.

Keep members informed on local, state, and national political issues concerning homeschooling.

How to Get Started

Once you've decided you want to be in a support group, you should research any established groups in your area to see if they will meet your needs. It is much easier to join an established group (or to make a sub-group) than it is to start a new one. Sub-groups can be just like the parent group, or they can have an individual need that they meet, such as a teen or preschool class, or a group that uses the same curriculum or is interested in the same outings.

It helps to join or start a group that has the same philosophies as you do, both educational and religious. I have found that having a stated purpose of intent, including those philosophies, makes it easier to know what the group is all about and it eliminates surprises and misunderstandings later.

After you've checked out the local groups, you may decide to start your own. Starting a new group can be a lot of work, but it can also be very rewarding. It helps to have a few people interested and committed to helping things get started. It's nice to start with a few friends, but if you're new to homeschooling (or to the area), this could be difficult. In this case you could ask the local support groups if they know anyone who may be interested in a new group or you could advertise in a local homeschool newsletter or the local newspaper.

The Planning Stage

You don't need a lot of people to get started. I think it is easier to start with 4-6 families and grow from there. It's nice to start with an informal meeting to get to know one another. You should discuss the needs of the people involved and get everyone thinking about the groups' formation. At this point you can get a feel for how organized things should be.

One way to get an idea of what everyone wants is to create a questionnaire. I feel that starting out by being organized and knowing what the group's intent and direction will be can help in the long run. It is much easier to organize in the beginning than later on.

At the next meeting, you will want to finalize the group's intent and purpose. This could be written out as a member's guide. Things you may want to include:

A stated purpose, such as "to provide a support group to homeschooling families by having a monthly meeting for parents and a monthly field trip for everyone."

A philosophy statement, such as "to have a group of open-minded people who focus on educational and social aspects of homeschooling." If you want families with the same religious background as yourself, make that part of your statement.

Name of the group. Sometimes this can be the hardest thing to come up with. Many groups use the name of the town or area they live in as part of their name. You could have a contest for the name and get the kids involved, too.

How organized do you want to be? Do you want regular meetings?

Where will they be? Do you want a newsletter? What about field trips? What about new members, etc. Support group jobs and who will do them: Many times one person ends up taking on all the jobs that need done at the beginning, so unless one person wants to do this, get volunteers early on! I feel that the more involved all the members are the better things will go. The level of organization everyone wants will determine how many jobs there will be. Some of the potential jobs include newsletter editor, group directory publisher, meeting planner, field trip planner, a welcome person for new members, someone to track and report on local legal issues and legislative matters, a special events coordinator, treasurer, and a phone tree contact person. You might start with some of these jobs and add others later.

You may want to have a requirement about member activity, such as a required number of meetings attended in order to stay an active member, or that everyone does a job for six months. You may want to charge for the newsletter or for a facility rental fee.

How big do you want the group to become? It may seem far off, but you never know how many homeschoolers may be looking for a group like yours.

Do you want an open membership or do you want to stay small and more intimate? You can set a number of families that you don't want to exceed, or, if your group gets too large, you may decide to reorganize into sub-groups or to split the group.

What Makes a Successful Support Group?

In your initial planning stages, keep in mind that one of the keys to success is how well the support group addresses the needs of its members. I have found that a key ingredient is some form of regular contact. This can be a contact person, regular meetings, or a newsletter. Most groups have all of these.

In our busy world, people can't always keep up with all that's going on. If you have regular meetings at the same time and place, even when only a few people attend, members will at least know they can count on the meetings being consistent. Even if they miss a meeting or two, they will know when the next one will be.

If you have a regular contact person, members can call this person to find out what is going on, or they can inform this person about events that others might be interested in. This contact person can initiate a phone tree, although I have found that phone trees are not always reliable.

I prefer a newsletter as primary contact. Members can send in dates and times for events that they plan. It is also fun to have members send in homeschooling tips or book reviews. Some newsletters even encourage the kids to send in articles and pictures.

The group I'm with has a regular planning meeting, where we plan out the next month's events and field trips and a newsletter is sent out with all the finalized information. This is convenient because not everyone can make the planning meetings and it's also nice to have the newsletter as a written reminder.

The people themselves make a group successful. If you have people who are committed to try and make it to all of the field trips, then there will be more cohesiveness, and finding people with similar interests is just nice. Once people make friends with one another they will go to more events to be with each other. Many times having kids the same ages and/or sex helps with the planning of activities. Family with young children have needs totally different from families with teens. Although I don't personally advocate age or sex segregated activities, there may be times when specific events require this.

It's also convenient to have members who live in close proximity. Sometimes a long drive for meetings can be a big deterrent.

How To Keep It Going

Each support group has an evolutionary process of its own. Many grow and become very successful, others stay small and tight knit. Some lose members and enthusiasm until they vanish. People change, and their needs change. If your group is to have a long life, it will need to change at some point.

It helps to not expect too much and to not take change too personally. Know that everyone needs a break at some point and some people just need to move on. Members have their own specific needs and they may need more or less than the support group has to offer. It's hard when people you've become good friends with move on, but there are more people out there for you to make friends with, to share ideas and grow with.

One thing that helps is to have a lot of people involved in the jobs so one person doesn't carry the load and get burned out. It's fun to change jobs around and to get new members interested in helping.

In summary, support groups can be anything you want them to be.

The more you are involved with them, the more you'll get out of them. I like things well organized, but if that doesn't fit your plans that's fine. I have learned a lot from my involvement with support groups, and you will too.

Your kids will meet some wonderful friends, and when people ask you that burning question all homeschoolers get asked about social-ization, you can calm many fears by simply talking about your support group.

Each member, including yourself, is an asset to the group. Each of us has a lot to share, be active and let others know your ideas. There is no one right way to homeschool—or to form a support group, so how can you go wrong?

If you've been thinking of joining or starting a support group, there's no time like the present. Good luck!

From the May-June, 1994 issue of *Home Education Magazine.*

The Making of a Network

Debbie Westheimer

The parent's meeting adjourned. Jerry pulled Wendy aside for a consultation on basket making. Wendy recently offered our Homeschool Network a workshop on basket making and Jerry was impressed. He was determined to make some baskets for Christmas, including an egg basket for his brother who owns a farm near by.

A group of moms and children gathered at a local community col-lege to watch a play put on by Artreach, a touring company from Cincinnati. This year's performance left us in a melancholy state. We watched *The Young Cherokee,* about the life of a Cherokee brave in the unspoiled grounds of North America. We witnessed the retelling of great myths and customs and went home wanting to know more of his culture.

Dick offered his musical talents to the parents of our Network. Sydney, a representative of Music for Little People, brought many an instrument, including a talking drum. Parents of our Network brought their home collections. All told we have two xylophones, two dulcimers, drums, guitars, a piano, a couple of autoharps and several shakers, bells, and sticks. We came together to make music. Many were surprised to find that *Skip To My Lou* banged out so smoothly, but the most pleasant arrangements were the improvisational scores that filled the air. We were all musicians that night. Hidden talents had been tapped. Parents who had never before felt comfortable with music as a doer were now inspired to share with their children.

All of these events took place among a group of families who had one thing in common. We all home educate our children and are members of The Homeschool Network of Greater Cincinnati. We have been an official group, complete with name and newsletter since the winter of 1990. We are relatively small, presently 35 families. Some of us are quite active, participating in offered events and helping with organizational duties. Others just read the newsletter and know that the phone directory is handy if ever support is needed. How did these families find each other? What is the making of a Network? Why choose to share the intimacy of homeschooling with a group outside ones own family?

My favorite personal story to tell regarding finding another family is how we met the Brauns. We operate a small food co-op out of our home and wanted to expand to receive a discount from the warehouse. In the spring of 1989, we put an ad in the paper and Karen Braun responded with interest. We shared some information about ourselves. I told her we lived on a farm. "Oh, really, we do to." I disclosed that my husband was a teacher. "Oh, really, mine is too." I confided that we are a homeschooling family. "Oh, really, we are too." We were thrilled to meet another family with whom we had so much in common. We have become close over the years and appreciate the friendship for our entire family.

Another source for contacts was a list of families in our area that were enrolled with Clonlara School's Home Based Education Program for homeschoolers. We enrolled with Clonlara in 1988. That first year we did enjoy the company of one other family on our list. The following year we were ready for more exposure. Certainly using the list was one way to form a Network. In our second year of homeschooling, we used the list to help us create "Open Home." We wanted to expand our contacts with area homeschoolers and at the same time stay put on our farm. We sent an invitation to all the families on our

contact list to join us twice a month for an unstructured play day. We
began in the fall of 1989. Occasionally our group organized activities
on these days. One Dad offered an orienteering course and rides in his
airplane. (We live near a county airport.) One crafty mom brought
magic markers for watercoloring and during the winter months she
taught us how to cut beautiful six sided snowflakes. During the celebration of Earth Week in the spring of 1990, we invited an herbalist
and edible plant specialist to our farm to lead us on a walk to identify the greenery. Most of the time though, "Open House" is just for
play.

While Clonlara provided our family with some names, most of our
contacts were made through the "ripple effect." Word slowly spread
that we had our children at home. We found that we were not alone
nor unique in our decision to home educate. Each organization or
group that we had in the past associated with held at least one family
that was already homeschooling or one that was soon to be. La Leche
League, Quaker Meeting, Temple, my homeopathic study group, the
Midwives' office, and friends, all seemed to hold a narrow population
of genuine interest. While we didn't proselytize homeschooling, clearly our family was experiencing a wonderful thing. Our enthusiasm
helped other families consider this option for their own.

After this loose association of people recognized that it was meeting
regularly and enjoying the company and sharing as a group, we decided to be an official support group. We gave ourselves a name. We
wrote a mission statement. Amy started our first newsletter. We printed a brochure. We wanted to introduce ourselves and lend support to
other families considering home education. We advertised our parents
meetings in the datebook section of our city's newspaper. We also sent
a letter to area Superintendents, suggesting that our group may be
used by families in their district. A local publication called *All About
Kids* interviewed our families at an "Open Home." The *Cincinnati
Post* featured an article about our family's experience homeschooling.

Our group grew from this exposure. The Homeschool Network
wanted recognition, not as a service organization, but rather as a support group for area homeschooling families. We wanted to let others
realize that while homeschooling may not be the answer for their family, it was an educational option that should be known. Yes, you may
homeschool your children. Yes, you may take responsibility for their
education by choosing to design your own program in your own
home.

In any one month there are about seven organized activities that families may participate in. Calico Theatre offers performances from area artists. Parent's meetings commence with a potluck meal and provide for uninterrupted social and business meetings. "Monday Moments" was set up as an opportunity for sharing skills and interests. Cake decorating, basket making, sign language, modern dance, beekeeping, and archeology, have all been offered during these times. Genny has offered an art class in her home once a month for 4 to 8 year olds. Susan and Karleen have organized a class for homeschoolers at the Cincinnati Zoo. Susan also inspired our group to start "Passport Days," families who choose may host a country in their home. The children have a world map to mark their adventures and a passport that gets stamped in each "country."

Activities are part of our group experiences. Our Network also offers a rich source of human resources. "Monday Moments" was conceived to tap these sources. There are other opportunities for sharing. There is Tammy, a musician and Waldorf trained teacher who offers a class each week in hand craft skills (knitting and crocheting), recorder music, and form drawing. There is Milan, an entomologist at the Cincinnati Zoo who offered a session of classes about insects. There are professional musicians and choreographers, video artists, weavers, teachers and farmers, La Leche League leaders, ministers, carpenters, writers, actors and actresses, lawyers, mail workers, engineers and full time stay at home moms and dads. We are a rich group!

Two tenets I appreciate most about our group are that all of our activities (excepting our Mom's Cabin Fever Gathering and parent meetings) are family events. Our philosophy sees learning as a process without definition or time. We are all learners. Also, there is no hierarchy. No one person or persons own the group. Anyone may offer an event. We've had stone soup parties, tie-dye workshops and Halloween parties. New Games Day, Kite Making and Flying and a Jewish Seder are some attractions we have to look forward to this spring. Also, anyone may bring a concern or query to a business meeting and may have full voice in the decision making process. The location of these meetings rotates and with that the role of facilitator.

What are the merits of sharing homeschooling with others? Why would a family choose to associate with others that have made the same decision? We have experienced homeschooling both ways. The first year we did not associate with a group. (At that time The Homeschool Network did not exist and while there are well organized

Christian groups in our city, our religious beliefs limited our involvement. To be a member of this group, one is required to sign a statement that one's family is Christian.) This first year was hard for us. We had a difficult transition from school to home, partly because we had a two year old at the time, but mainly because I compared and expected our home to be like Dick's classroom. Knowing no other way, we brought school into our home. I am not so sure we would have used a group or its offered activities because we needed this time to find ourselves. What I wish we had at that time was the directory and mentor program that our Network now offers its members. I would have liked to call someone and say, "This isn't working; how can we change our routine to satisfy all that needs to be done?" While we did get answers for ourselves, it might have been nice to learn from others' mistakes.

Learning with and from a group is a nicety but Dick and I wanted just plain company. We also wanted our children to have exposure to other homeschoolers to help them establish a primary peer group outside their sibling relationship. While scouting and sports provide for community friendship, the Network loyalties seem deeper because the kids have a basic commonality. Schooling at home unites all age groups in ways that are hard to find anywhere else excepting the extended family: aunts, uncles, and cousins.

Our Network has become family in many respects by just being there. It has helped our entire family find satisfaction with our decision to school at home. Now, paradoxically, our challenge is to limit the amount of involvement we have in both activities and organizational charges. We want the older children to have time to explore the farm and their personal interests. We don't want to spend our time in the car; memories are vivid of our private school era: three years of driving, driving, driving. This fall, at a family meeting, we gave our kids the choice to do either the zoo class or the circle group (the Waldorf inspired class). While the zoo class is a wonderful experience (we know from participating in two fall sessions), we decided to try circle group this year. We simply didn't want to make the same mistakes we made the first year by overscheduling our calendar. The Network events are there if we choose to use them. The directory is there if we need to call on a friend. The newsletter is there to keep us informed and updated on issues pertaining to our group. I for one am glad for the choices and support for a Network that is there.

From the March-April, 1992 issue of *Home Education Magazine*.

Why The National Homeschool Association?

Dick Westheimer

Addendum to the third edition: The National Homeschool Association voluntarily disbanded itself in the fall of 2000.

"Why should we join the NHA? Our community homeschooling network serves our needs adequately." The first time I heard that question, it was from my very reasoned wife, Debbie. "We work hard enough to nurture our local contacts. What does this NHA do, anyway?"

Since that conversation (at which time I didn't have an adequate answer), I've heard the same question posed by others in a variety of ways, asked as often as I talk about the work of the National Homeschool Association. As the NHA has grown, and as I have come to work more closely with the organization, I've become better able to respond to such inquiries. Not only do I now know what the NHA does, but I recognize the importance of membership for our family and for others.

The NHA formed, as its statement of purpose affirms, "to advocate individual choice and freedom in education, to serve those families who choose to homeschool, and to inform the general public about home education." Few of us would doubt the importance of this work. Many, however, have meaningful concerns as to how to carry out such a vision. Homeschooling is essentially a grassroots activity. It flourishes when individual families consciously choose to step outside the mass educational system. It is at once a purely individual and a vigorously political activity that is best supported by working with those in ones own community. The "movement" thrives when families support each other and, when necessary, collaborate to work with regulatory and legislative bodies to establish and maintain the freedom to homeschool.

How the NHA Helps

How can a national homeschooling organization, such as the NHA, contribute to such grassroots work? The answer to this question lies at the heart of why the NHA is an important organizational commitment for homeschoolers. The NHA is carefully structured to keep and nourish the strength of homeschooling at the state and local level. As a national group it can facilitate local strength and effectiveness in a variety of ways:

1. Referrals: The NHA office receives thousands of phone calls each year asking for information about homeschooling. Most of these calls originate from new or prospective homeschoolers in need of support regarding their decision to home educate. The NHA responds by referring callers back to local and state contacts for assistance. Callers are encouraged to contact and work with homeschoolers close to home.

The office maintains a file of local and statewide support networks, groups affiliated with specific religious denominations, and those that serve families with special needs. When possible, callers are given several references. This file, however, needs constant updating and refinement, and should include the support groups that you work with. The NHA can most effectively refer homeschoolers (and others interested in information about home education) back to the "grassroots" if it has the names and descriptions of as many local and statewide groups as possible.

2. Information Dissemination: Occasionally we are faced with apparent crises regarding our right to homeschool. In order to make wise choices in these circumstances we need accurate, balanced information. Sometimes the (tale-bearing) counsel of self appointed "leaders" who purport to speak for all homeschooling families tells only part of the story necessary for us to make informed decisions. An organization such as the NHA allows those with varied but informed views about pertinent issues to have a forum by which to share those views. It is the role of an inclusive group such as the NHA to facilitate the flow of wise counsel among the only legitimate homeschooling "experts" - homeschoolers themselves.

3. Network building: The freedom to homeschool is best promoted when home educators from varied perspectives work together. The NHA can further the building of networks of homeschoolers in a number of ways. It has begun to convene regional conferences that bring people together to talk over perennial homeschooling issues. This fledgling effort has facilitated the exchange of information and ideas among homeschoolers and has energized those working to sustain local and statewide networks.

In addition, the *NHA Forum*, a quarterly newsletter, is growing to include contributions from the newsletters of state and local home-schooling organizations around the country. The *Forum* exchanges newsletters with close to one hundred local groups. From these newsletters, the *Forum* editors glean articles that contribute to a particular issue's discussion topic. In the future, the *Forum* plans to include a regular column that addresses families' actions in response to threats to homeschooling freedoms. Once again, this column would be comprised of articles excerpted from the exchange of newsletters the NHA receives.

Why Membership is Important

Undoubtedly membership in the NHA cannot supplant the role of the local support groups: the NHA does not have direct impact on the practical quality of ones homeschooling. Daily concerns such as curriculum and social contacts, housework and apprenticeships can best be dealt with in conversation with friends and community members. Regulatory obstacles most often occur at the local or statewide level and can best be addressed by homeschoolers working together at the grassroots.

Nonetheless, our family, among many others, has definite reasons for joining the National Homeschool Association. First, we emphatically want to support the broad-based free exchange of ideas fostered by the NHA. The Association gives voice, in its Forum, conferences, and Council, to a wide range of homeschoolers expressing diverse and important views about home education. When issues arise in need of consideration I know that NHA people will openly and cogently discuss the range of options that should be considered.

Secondly, the NHA is a democratically run national homeschooling organization. It is wholly open to all homeschoolers. All Council meetings are open to all members. The agenda of the organization is determined by the membership. Because of these qualities, the NHA can, with the participation of its members, facilitate the formation of coalitions of other homeschooling groups. Members can voice their opinions in the public arena as broadly informed constituents of an open, democratic organization - not as "spokespersons" for an exclusionary, special interest, enterprise. We can stand ready, if the need arises, to speak loudly and clearly with the many voices of the home-schooling community, in defense of the freedom to homeschool.

Membership strengthens the NHA by broadening the base of support for this work. Both the knowledge we bring to the "conversation" and our membership dollars contribute to its vitality. As our numbers grow, we can convene more regional conferences, nurture more people into assuming advocacy roles at the local, regional, and national level, and staff the office to assist, in a more timely manner, those seeking support or advice.

What You Can Do

1. Let the NHA office know about the local and statewide homeschooling organizations that you belong to. Include the name, address, metropolitan region if appropriate, contact telephone number, focus, and any distinguishing characteristics. The office fields thousands of inquiries each year. Almost all of these are referred directly back to local support groups.

2. Encourage your local or state support group newsletter editor to exchange subscriptions with the *NHA Forum*. The information shared within your group might help others in their efforts to homeschool.

3. Become a member. Join with others' efforts to "advocate individual choice and freedom in education." Your voice and your membership dollars contribute to the working resources of the NHA (annual family membership is $15.00).

4. Attend, help convene, contribute your experience to a regional or national NHA conference. We are made stronger by the number of people who share and build on a discussion of the issues fundamental to sustaining our freedoms and responsibilities as homeschoolers.

Addendum to the third edition: The National Homeschool Association voluntarily disbanded itself in the fall of 2000.

From the May-June, 1994 issue of *Home Education Magazine*.

PERSONAL EXPERIENCE

Part Six

Adjusting to Freedom

Tom Friedlander

When my wife and I first considered teaching our own kids we did so with grave reservations, most of which were overcome by reading the home schooling books of Raymond and Dorothy Moore. We were in the midst of many changes at the time, and so were prepared for what seemed to be another logical step in growing together as a family. Cathy and I decided to go whole hog in teaching our own, not subscribing to an outside curriculum, but purchasing simple workbooks from a nearby teaching supply store.

We soon found that even these workbooks were holding our oldest back from learning instead of assisting her. It became frustrating for my wife to have to slow Becky down to the pace of the workbooks. Cautiously at first, then with unmasked joy, we rid ourselves of the limitations which the outside teaching materials imposed on us. Immediately we saw Becky start to grasp concepts at a rate which surpassed even our highest expectations. Of course, this change involved somewhat more planning for Cathy, but as she was now in total charge of the schooling environment this became a joyful and satisfying challenge to her.

Last year a more subtle change occurred in our home schooling philosophy, but one that was to have no less of an impact. We found the emphasis almost imperceptibly changing from our teaching Becky (and now Caleb) to the children learning more and more of their own volition; from pushing our head knowledge at the kids to their pulling useful skills from us in satisfying their curiosity.

Within a school term Becky had progressed so far that we could realistically see that if she continued learning at her present rate her formal education would be complete in a few years (mind you, this is a seven year old we're talking about). As the term drew to a close we began asking ourselves questions. What were the limits of basic knowledge that we wanted to have the kids know which would not only satisfy state requirements but, more importantly, equip them with the skills Cathy and I feel are essential for them to succeed in life? Without a standard curriculum, what would we teach them in the next decade or so (Wisconsin mandates the education of children until they are sixteen years of age) without schooling them to death?

So began the second period of questioning in our home schooling venture (the first being before we actually began teaching Becky), and, although we had now gotten our feet wet, it was no less a dilemma for us than before we began. At one point we were seriously considering entering them in the public school system. The thing that kept us going was the knowledge that traditional schooling, at best, could not duplicate what we were doing, and sending the kids to public or private school would almost certainly result in their spiritual, moral, social, and intellectual regression.

I think many home schoolers have reached this point. With a couple of years of unschooling behind them they now feel comfortable as parent teachers, and now wish to more fully test out the freedoms of education. The peripheral questions of home education have already been settled in these parents' minds, but, especially if they are currently subscribing to a curriculum, they have never really needed to ponder how much or to what extent they should teach. The parent teachers now wish to more fully test out the promises that previously drew them to consider home education. They wish to see their children's curiosity lead them to knowledge that will stick, even within the confines of their present curriculum. To do so, these parent teachers must satisfy themselves that their child's curiosity will enable them to learn the basics, achieving and even excelling academically while at the same time satisfying state and local educational guidelines for home education. Possibly they have caught a glimpse of what the kids could learn if given more freedom. Or it could be that the curriculum, for all it's excellence, is no longer working out. Perhaps, like us, the parents simply wonder if it would not be simpler without the financial load and restrictions of a standard curriculum.

For us, the extent of the preparation that our children receive will be determined ultimately by experience, and no doubt will be different for each of our three children. Our kids will learn much of what is required through pursuit of his or her own interests and specialties.

Yet even this knowledge was not fully satisfactory to us. We had to be certain that our kids had certain basic life skills, even before pursuing their own areas of giftings. Pondering this, we allowed ourselves to think in terms of the six (for the most part) logical areas of study which the state of Wisconsin divided mandated curriculum into: reading, language arts, mathematics, social studies, science, and health. We then attempted to define these areas in terms of the specific skills that we wished our eldest to have, afterwards breaking these skills into easily teachable concepts.

For instance, in the area of math we wanted Becky to (among other things) balance a checkbook. This means she will have to add and subtract columns of at least five digit figures, as well as be comfortable working with two digit decimals. After mastery of this, we will introduce her to simple calculator skills, and teach her how to unscramble a checking account statement.

Admittedly, practical skills to be learned in the area of social studies are hard to pinpoint. But even this relatively large field becomes less vague when broken down into smaller sub-sections (civics, economics, geography, sociology, etc.). And normally, most of the important knowledge which kids learn in these areas is through living experiences or by reading (which we are deep believers in) rather than by sit down teaching.

We now see that the promises of our home teaching were best realized when the structure and curriculum contained a great amount of flexibility. It is essential that we not become over involved with the theory and mechanics of parent teaching. It is in play, channelled with the proper amount of parental guidance, that our children learn most of what they have to. We are continually amazed at the flexibility and adaptability of our schooling. It seems that the more we move toward unstructured teaching, the greater motivation our children have to learn.

It helps not to be presumptuous of our educational freedoms. Our state and our local school district are not exactly supportive of semi-structured schooling, but neither are they prohibitive. Cathy's schooling records are immaculate, detailed almost to the point of absurdity. We keep informed of what is happening with other home schoolers in our area and in the state, and with the legislative and judicial climate. We are still growing and learning, changing in homeschool theory and practice. This is how it should be. The more we grow, the more we venture into unknown territory, but the smoother parent teaching seems to flow. Cathy and I, like most home schoolers, have seen that the benefits of home schooling are more than worth the supposed risks we are taking with our children's lives.

What do we propose for the future? We are learning to move gracefully from a curriculum centered education to one semi-based on our offspring's curiosity. And, as I mentioned earlier, we plan to eventually channel our threesome's education around their interests, giftings, and skills.

We are fast learning that the supposed elements of risk in letting our kids go, to learn as they may, can be regulated by the parent teacher. We who teach our own are not simply substituting one method of education for another, but are involving more of our children's curiosity in their learning adventures.

From the September, 1987 issue of *Home Education Magazine*.

Winter Homeschooling

Helen Hegener

The holiday season has always been my very favorite time of the year. I prefer the slower pace of life in winter, with wonderful smells from the kitchen, the sounds of children and dogs playing in the snow. I like the crisp clear days, the beauty of a freshly-fallen snow, the star-bright nights. But mostly I enjoy this time of the year because that's when families gather together in thankfulness and celebration.

In the summertime children always seem so busy and occupied with important doings and their enthusiastic enjoyment of absolutely everything. Take them to the beach and they're off swimming and collecting stuff and meeting new friends and building castles in the sand. Take them on a picnic and they're off as quickly as they can pile out of the car, looking for neat rocks and scary snakes and who-knows-what-else. Oh, they'll show up when the cooler and the picnic basket are unpacked, but then they're gone again, skipping through the creek. Even at home there's so much to do: running and bicycling and playing in the sprinklers and swinging and so much more...

Then in late fall the pace slows, the kids start lingering inside later in the mornings, reading a book or building a model. They'll still race through the day - there's so much to do and like the squirrels they seem to know that winter's coming - but in the evenings, instead of dashing off for a game of hide-and-seek in the evening shadows, they might decide to play a game, or they'll slip a movie into the VCR, or they'll gather ingredients and bake a few cookies.

And then winter! Winter means snuggling up with a good book, having plenty of time to spend on a craft or a hobby, writing letters, trying out a new recipe. Winter is a time for coming close again, a time for families to build those reserves of strength that are needed when life becomes more hectic again.

This is the time of year when homeschooling seems like the only reasonable and sensible way to raise children. Instead of walking to school or the bus stop in freezing temperatures, the kids will heatedly argue over the right way to pronounce a six syllable word. Instead of trooping into classrooms with thirty other kids their ages, the older kids will teach the younger kids the fine art of making golden brown pancakes. No bells or buzzers regulate the day, no playground bullies spark fear, no teachers frown at forgotten homework or a temporary lapse of attention.

Homeschooling gives children time to learn what they want to know at their own pace, in their own way. Homeschooling encourages digging deeper, asking more questions, understanding more fully. And homeschooling challenges the status quo, the institution, and the fast lane mode of thinking.

Homeschooling gives a family a different outlook on life. It removes the dependence on institutional expertise, reaffirms the capability of individuals, restores confidence in the ability and the need to be responsible for one's own life, and for one's own family. It allows the gentle rhythms of family life to flow uninterrupted, it gives kids and parents time to really get to know each other, to intimately understand how relationships between people work.

In this slowing-down, turning inward, mellowing time of the year, as we cuddle in bed and read an old favorite story for the fiftieth time, as we wrap big and small hands around cups of steaming cocoa, as we sprawl on the floor to help assemble a jigsaw puzzle, let us remember that as homeschooling families, we have much to be thankful for and to celebrate.

From the November-December, 1991 issue of *Home Education Magazine.*

Five Years of Homeschooling

Sue Thompson

When our first child, Grace, was born, I was sure I wanted to home school her. I had very idealistic expectations of what our home school would be like. My kids would receive everything I had never received from my own education — freedom, inspiration, unlimited variety, meaningful experiences and useful skills. Little Grace was eager to learn everything and I was anxious to teach her as much as possible. By the time she was three she was reading from a first grade reader; beginning to learn about cooking, sewing and carpentry; could identify many local trees, birds, and seashells; and was good at drawing and helping with housework as well as taking care of her new sister, Hanna.

But after Hanna's birth our learning experiences changed from unlimited potential to just getting through each day and keeping everything together. About this time Grace began to look forward to kindergarten. I had always said she was free to go to school if she wanted to, and so it was agreed. During this time all school type learning at home stopped. Grace was planning on kindergarten, she wasn't interested in reading lessons, and it seemed I had no spare time anyway. Kindergarten was a big disappointment for Grace. Within a few weeks she was complaining daily about her teacher, who said drawings had to be done in a certain way, houses could not be multicolored, and children should not have a drink of water except at recess. The teacher did not appreciate having a student like Grace, who, in the middle of an "all plants need soil" lecture, pointed out that algae and mildew don't. She didn't appreciate this student who, in the middle of an Indian paddling song, explained that, "If we only paddle on one side like you tell us, the canoe will go in a circle!" So, after about three months of this, Grace became a kindergarten dropout. We were both delighted with the decision. (Surprisingly, the school never questioned us about this. But we lived on a boat at the time, so perhaps they assumed we had just sailed away.)

All the other boat families used (and praised) Calvert School courses, so we ordered Calvert's first grade course, which arrived in a big box complete with books, workbooks, teacher's manual, pencils, erasers, crayons, rulers, scissors, index cards, and five kinds of paper.

The beginning of first grade was a breeze for Grace. Letter names, counting, matching sets — we raced through several lessons each day. When we arrived at the point where the material was new we slowed to one lesson per day.

The lessons were fun. Calvert's teacher's manuals specify exactly what work is to be covered each day in each subject. It is very structured, even to the point of telling teachers what questions to ask: "Point to the word 'gift' at the top of the page and ask what letter the word begins with." But I appreciated this structure now that I actually had the responsibility of my child's education. I wanted to make sure that we fulfilled or exceeded state requirements in case we ever got caught. (Prior to 1985, when home schooling was legalized in Florida, this was often on my mind.) I also now had the added job of another baby, Bucko, and so our formal schooling became limited to just completing each lesson as efficiently as possible.

Calvert School has a Teacher's Advisory Service to which you can send all the student's tests to be evaluated by a teacher in their Baltimore school. We decided to pay for this extra service for Grace's second grade, partly because of pressure from relatives and partly because I wasn't sure if I was doing everything right — Grace seemed to be having a little trouble reading. With the Calvert teacher's corrections Grace learned to form her letters perfectly and I was assured that her reading was up to par, even though she often hesitated and forgot words in her reading assignments. Meanwhile, I decided it was time for three year old Hanna to start first grade. Hanna was very bright and somewhat hyperactive and I sensed she needed to be channeled into something useful that would help her feel good about herself. So we started her on school. We did not breeze through the beginning as with Grace. This was all new to her, and we went quite slowly, often going weeks without a new lesson, until I was sure she knew and could write all the numbers and letters.

I should also mention at this point the tribulations of having a toddler around and the endless interruptions for crying or diaper changing. Trying to keep it all together was a major challenge! Bucko scribbled in the schoolbooks, ripped compositions, and lost the pencils. I would nurse him while one of the girls was reading and he'd finally fall asleep and... ah, now we could continue.

Hanna caught on to the school work and surprised me with her ability to read. The stories that six year old Grace had called boring were very interesting to a three year old. She enjoyed reading the stories over and over. Math was harder for her, she could barely sit still long enough for it.

The next fall, Grace started third and Hanna started second grade. We did not use the Teacher's Advisory service that year, the cost for two students was just beyond our range. This was the year that the difference between Grace and Hanna became apparent. Hanna was not at all neat compared to Grace. But Hanna was only five, so I did not insist. She also took longer to grasp mathematical principles. To Grace, the logic of math was readily apparent. Hanna needed a lot of explaining. But reading was a different story. Compared to Grace, Hanna was a whiz at reading. She'd read her required story and then go on to the next and the next.

We settled into a routine, but it was not exactly pleasant. To be honest, the girls began to think schoolwork was a drag. We were doing it just to get it over with. What had happened to those ideals — the freedom, inspiration, and meaningful experiences? That year seemed to be a very untogether period in my life. The house was often a total mess, Bucko was often in trouble or nowhere to be seen, and the girls were often complaining about their schoolwork. I'd often get so frustrated with their balking that I'd threaten to send them to school. As a matter of fact, I began to think they might be better off in school. I reasoned that they would never act like this in school. They wouldn't groan or moan or refuse to do their work. They were taking ballet and gymnastics lessons and in those classes they were so polite and eager to learn. Why couldn't they be like that with me? Actually, things were not totally hopeless or I'm sure I would have sent them off to school. We did all believe in what we were doing.

That summer, I was pregnant again and we took a camping trip across the country to Washington state. This gave us all a much needed change of atmosphere and time to think about our lives. I saw how the years were slipping by without enough of the meaningful accomplishments I had envisioned. I imagined our kids growing into teenage misfits without my ever having discovered The Secret of Doing Everything Right.

I should mention my husband, Don, at this point. He was very encouraging and supportive. He believed I was doing a great job with the schooling and he would point out how well the girls had progressed. So, with his help, I was able to maintain my perspective and work to improve our home school.

We arrived home from our trip late in November. Grace was very anxious to start fourth grade. She wanted to get ahead and she worked hard most of the year. For Hanna, however, third grade was pretty boring. It wasn't much fun to teach her and I spent a lot of time wondering how to improve the situation. Reading continued to be her strong point. She would lose herself in books. She was also very good at spelling, and I attributed this to her extensive reading. Grace didn't enjoy reading and her spelling was atrocious. To encourage her to read I provided her with lots of books that interested her, and I could see her reading improve daily as a result, but spelling remained a problem for her. We went through a phase of writing each misspelled word ten times and then using them in sentences. She would learn the word, but forget it later when she used it in a composition.

Compositions! What a tribulation they became! Calvert School assigns lots of compositions — two to three each week. Both girls, in my opinion, were good at writing and I thought their compositions were delightful, but they hated it! They would do anything to get out of writing compositions, so I began to think up alternatives. Hanna enjoyed "finishing sentences." I would write the first word or words of about ten sentences which she would complete. Grace preferred writing poetry, and she wrote quite a few nice ones — she even decorated and illustrated them.

The birth of Gabriel was a wonderful occasion for all of us. He was our third home birth, an event shared by all the children, who have loved him intensely ever since. Grace's birthday was the next morning and she didn't even mind baking her own birthday cake. And neither girl minded taking two weeks off from school lessons!

This past summer I made a real commitment to constant improvement in my teaching — which meant making the lessons more fun, interesting, and meaningful. It meant changing the format whenever necessary and letting the kids make choices and discipline themselves. It meant true democratic agreements. Grace, age ten, decided to do lessons all summer so she could start fifth grade before fall school started. Hanna, age seven, chose a one month vacation and began fourth grade in August. Bucko turned five this summer and Grace thought he was ready for first grade. I didn't agree initially, arguing that he was too contrary and moody. But he was anxious to learn, so we tried it out. He just loves it! He is eager and polite and inspired, and I am delighted — and very careful to nurture this precious attitude! For Bucko, we never go on to the next lesson if he hasn't mastered the material or if he isn't enjoying it. I am careful to listen to all of his comments no matter how irrelevant they may seem. If he wants to do work not in the lesson, I check my impulse to say "Let's get done with the lesson first," and let him learn in his own way.

The girls, too, are learning in their own ways. For example, Grace corrects her own daily spelling lessons and uses her own method to study the misspellings. And she is really improving. Hanna prefers to be told the correct spelling immediately, whereupon she erases the word and rewrites it. She doesn't like to leave any mistakes showing. She is still a whiz at reading, she recently read all the C. S. Lewis books in two weeks. This year, she's read Tolkien, all of the McGuffey readers and countless piles of books from the library.

Required compositions have been completely eliminated. I know the girls are good writers and will write when they have the urge to. In place of compositions we now have writing games like puzzle sentences, treasure hunts, word games and relay stories, and this has made writing challenging and fun. In math we have agreed that if they show they know the material well, they only need to do a few problems instead of whole pages. Because of this they are more careful and precise with their calculations.

Their schoolwork is all done in the mornings, which gives them time to develop their own interests and have fun. The girls have built a huge dollhouse which fills half the kids' room. It is inhabited by their many little children dolls with which they spend hours playing — the stories they develop are superior to any compositions! Grace recently took a CPR course at her own insistence and she and Hanna entered a local art festival. Hanna won an honorable mention for a life size doll she made, and Grace's drawings were so good that the judges mistakenly grouped her work with the Jr. High level and gave her third prize!

As for me, the rewards are without measure. I can really enjoy the lessons, and I learn a lot, too. It no longer matters to me if I don't do everything right. I no longer feel defeated if Hanna won't do her math or if the baby throws a tantrum in the middle of a history lesson. I know I now have the gist of what's important — that's an attitude and a belief in my kids — and from that point on, we can accomplish our goals.

From the February, 1986 issue of *Home Education Magazine*.

Homeschool Confidential

Steve Thom

Home schooling was one of my many brainstorms. And like most men, I thought it was a pretty brilliant idea, thank you. I became obsessed. The postal service and Mountain Bell assigned their best people to my case. How-to books, brochures, catalogs, calendars, correspondence schools, curriculum tapes, case histories; I sent for 'em all. It made a lot of sense. This is God's plan for the family. The public schools are failing in their mission. The "experts" all agree that home schooling is the wave of the future. There are even uneducated kids going to Harvard. That's the Ivy League, fer cryin' out loud!

So all we need is a plan. I'm a great planner. Execution isn't my strong point, but I can plan. Well, first of all we need a correspondence school. Yeah, that's the ticket; nothing too radical the first year. This is, after all, school, so let's act like a school. Lots of pages of math problems and drilling. And lots of scripture reading and that kind of stuff, since this is a Christian school. Now, all we need is a teacher, hmmmmm. Oh, yeah, my wife Marcia is right here. Everything I've read says that the wife does all, er, excuse me, most of the teaching. Perfect. Okay everybody, let's do it!

Well, contrary to the rosy home schooling experiences of everyone else on the planet Earth, our first year was gruesome. I assumed that once people understood why we wanted to teach our children, and they would understand, we would be raised upon the shoulders of perfect strangers and carried off into a glowing sunset. Oh, yeah. People do not understand. Many do not want to understand. Most get that glazed look so often seen during home movie screenings. Any explanation of motivation for home education is regarded as criticism of those who do not choose to do so. And then there are relatives, or should I say grandparents. And teachers. And members of the church. And everyone else. Now when someone asks, "So how's the home schooling going?", we say, "Fine." When somebody asks "How are you?", they really don't want to hear all about your athlete's foot. Home schooling is the same. The answer is "Fine, thank you."

Well, it really doesn't matter what the rest of Western culture thinks. God is with us. We teach from the Bible. The workbooks quote from scripture. We sing hymns. We memorize from the Bible.

We've got it made, right? Oh, yeah. Believe it or not, the single great-est example of literature, the Bible, can be made boring. Now I know God is with us. But we live the Bible, too. And our speech, our behav-ior, our example, our walk are the things that our children learn from the most. And our behavior bordered on the bizarre.

I would saunter in from work at 10:30 p.m. and Marcia would look like a zombie. She was wiped out, done in, drained. She couldn't do it. Three children ages 7, 3, and 1 1/2 add up to a lot more than any unarmed 37 year old adult. Marcia felt guilty because she couldn't teach one child, chase another, nourish a third, run a household, and work part-time. Can you imagine? Well, I knew she needed help, and needed it fast. So, you know what I did? I told her, without any hesi-tation, "It'll get better." Case closed. After all, that's what all the books said.

We finally decided that this was simply not working. We bailed out of the borrrring correspondence school. We began to do fun stuff. You know, it's possible to enjoy learning. In fact, that's probably the only way to learn. Boy, times sure have changed. Most importantly, we learned to relax. We found a program that suits us just fine. Don't get me wrong. It's not all peaches and cream. The kids still clobber each other, have to be reminded to do their chores a zillion times a day, argue, whine, mope, wheedle, and duke it out. But it's a whole lot bet-ter. And we're better. And now they're really learning about God, and love, and sharing, and patience, and learning. And I help too. Sorta.

So — whaddya say we stop painting this Pollyanna picture of home schooling. That kind of propaganda is fine for school boards and rel-atives. But people who are really considering home education need the truth. Nothin' but the facts, Ma'am. Sure, it's great for the family in the long run, but sometimes it's the pits. I just love some of the stuff you read about home schooling: "The mother should take some time just for herself every day . The parents should have a night out togeth-er, by themselves, at least once a week." Wonderful. Great. Will the authors please take a number and wait outside our front door? Or the home educator who describes himself as having a sense of humor, being literate, patient, and confident. Fine. Good. Would all the nor-mal human beings line up to the left and begin feeling intensely guilty, thank you.

Don't get me wrong. I believe in home schooling. I love having my children around. I believe that this is part of God's plan for the fami-ly. I have an even greater love and regard for my wife than I did before.

In spite of the first year, I enjoy home schooling. But let's be honest. Teaching your children at home is very hard work. It can be disruptive. Nobody's going to put their thumb in a pie and say, "What a good boy you are." There are plenty of good days and there are many lousy days. And it can't be a cheap imitation of public school.

A recent letter from our current program says it best: "Many parents, after a trial period of 'school at home,' have done one of two things: either given up entirely in discouragement, or used books more creatively and watched their program blossom into an exciting new home school."

And remember what I always say: "It'll get better!"

From the August, 1986 issue of *Home Education Magazine*.

A Place of Their Own

Linda Dobson

Luckily, I made a lot of mistakes when I started to homeschool. Yes, luckily. For in discovering what homeschool isn't, I uncovered the inherent potential of our Rainbow Holistic School.

My first and nearly fatal mistake was attempting to duplicate the classrooms of my own childhood; a specific time for this, a certain way to accomplish that. And heaven forbid I didn't squeeze in at least a few math problems every day! Then one fateful afternoon, I actually fell asleep while preparing the following day's lesson plan. I vowed never to impose such drudgery on Charles, my only student, again.

But the following year when Erika, student #2, entered kindergarten, I watched helplessly as history repeated itself. Her initial enthusiam deteriorated into quiet resignation; an acceptance of school as one of life's inevitable chores. In my struggle to reach the stars, I didn't realize that navigating with a public school curriculum was akin to traveling there by way of Cleveland - in a Chevy!

A curriculum does not a school make, but I stubbornly continued along the only route I knew, attempting to "spice up" the curriculum in an ever-failing attempt to make school more "fun."

The self-imposed stress of outrageous expectations, coupled with that of abject failure, forced me into a subconscious hiatus. And the less I worried and planned, the more Charles and Erika responsibly assumed control of their day. They had inadvertently discovered a more direct route to my lofty goal. The school had to be a place of their own. There existed a fundamental difference between their route and mine. Typical schooling is imposed from without, while proper schooling should emerge from within. A homeschool is not created for the children, but of the children. Although obliged to follow some sort of curriculum, it is a place tailored to fit the children it serves, not vice versa. It's a place where young minds may inquire freely, where individual interests flourish, where childen learn at their own pace. One night's simple realization for me; a new dawn for Rainbow Holistic School.

I spent that wonderful evening assessing our dining room turned schoolroom. It appeared to have been transferred directly from the local school: neat rows of books, a shiny globe, and a world map reflected the room's purpose. The green chalkboard stared back blankly, awaiting my interpretation of the following day's lessons. Too bad: there would be no lessons tommorrow.

Charles and Erika whooped and cheered at the announcement the next morning, then seriously pondered the question, "How can we change this room to make it a nicer place?"

We commenced a remodeling project immediately. Although we kept all the basics, their places of honor were usurped by more personal belongings. Charles wanted our parakeet in the room; we moved the globe. Erika disliked trudging to the attic for the scrap box each time she desired to undertake a much-loved art project, so the corner bookcase found a new home in the front room. The scrap box is now as accessable as her creative ideas.

"What else don't you like about the room, gang?" I asked, eager to please.

"What I'd really like," Erika answered, "Is to be able to reach the shelves myself."

By relocating the shelves lower on the walls, even Adam, the preschooler, can easily help himself to anything he wants. We gained precious wall space, quickly filled with Charles' favorite planet poster and hanging skeleton model. Erika contributed her recent, painstakingly completed needlepoint project, and suggested we hang a few special photographs from our recent trip to Montreal. Adam returned from the kitchen with a favorite doggy mug to hold pens and pencils on the work table.

Although tired and hungry by noon, we delighted in the results of our work. After a lunch devoured in record time, all three children hurried back into their room to touch, explore, and independently settle down to paint. Each completed a couple of pages of math, to boot!

A relaxed attitude and a new sense of space contributed greatly to work completed, both in quantity and quality. But I sensed the school, although a comfortable room in which to be, was still merely a place in the house. An inspired holistic approach to education required still more of the school, and of me.

The school should occupy a place in the heart. A physical place may be special, but it's the emotional ties that bind. A physical place may be comfortable, but a true sense of belonging emanates from within. After a democratic vote, blue and white became our school colors. Art class yielded a newly designed and colorful school flag. And our school song, like other contents of the heart, is readily available everywhere. Written to the tune of "You're a Grand Old Flag," the song echoes loudly whether we're taking a trip to town or hiking through the woods.

As a celebration of our emancipation from a school calendar, we now create our own holidays. Whether celebrating "Kitty Cat Day" upon adopting an abandoned kitten, "Jack Frost Holiday" when we wake to find the lawn sparkling in the fall, or "National Magic Week" in respect to the kids' favorite theatre, the anticipation of a day integrating personal interests and scholastic pursuits awakens sleepy minds.

However, my children's minds are rarely sleepy anymore. They are, instead, filled with anticipation and wonder. After two years of trial and error, the true light of homeschooling shines through, for I have learned to live in their world, and what a wonderful world it is!

Unfortunately, it is hard to understand, and harder to accept that, under normal circumstances, society forces adults to live in a world far removed from our children. We become comfortable with pattern and habits; children thrive on novelty. Our day overflows with obligations; theirs with delight. While we worry about tommorrow our children are busy living today.

Yes, it is our knowledge of a better way that allows the seed, the idea of a preferable school, to grow. It is our action that transforms the idea into reality. But it is the reflection of all that is our children that causes it to be what it naturally should be: a place of their own.

From the January-February, 1988 issue of *Home Education Magazine.*

Testing in the Real World

Mark & Helen Hegener

Our daughter Jody, 12, passes the time while we're washing dishes or driving to town by asking us to think up words for her to spell. She insists that we give her at least two chances to get each word right before telling her the correct spelling. She often asks why words are spelled the way they are, wants us to point out words which sound alike but have different spellings, and she likes to have words that she's missed before reintroduced in later games. For the past few weeks she's asked to play this game at every opportunity, and her brothers, never very interested in orthography, are now challenging her with their increasing spelling skills.

Our youngest sons, Michael and Christopher, ages 6 and 10, often play little games such as "Can we name all fifty states?" or "Who invented the ...," or they'll try to name all of the colors of the spectrum in order. Sometimes they'll quiz us or their two older brothers, wanting to know if we can spell words like 'aluminum' or 'university,' or if we can name the dates of certain historic wars or presidential terms, or if we know whether an armadillo is a reptile or a mammal.

We suppose one could say that they're testing themselves with these little games. But they are always so eager to play these games, and they take them so seriously and spend so much time 'brushing up" so that they can do better the next time around, that it's difficult for us to consider them tests in the traditional sense. To the kids, the spelling and geography games they've invented are just pleasant little challenges. It's something they enjoy doing, much like playing tag or hide and seek. And yet these games do fit the dictionary definition of a test: "an examination for determining what students have learned about a particular subject."

Tests come in many shapes and sizes, they're given for many reasons, and the way a person perceives testing is shaped by his experience with tests. Our children have never been tested in the traditional sense for one simple reason: we trust them to learn what they need to know. They're intelligent children well aware of what it takes for their parents to get along in this world. We know that they understand that this includes the basics; to read to write to spell and to do math. They take these basic skills quite seriously and each one has gone about learning them with a self-styled dedication and perseverance. They realize that mastery of these and other skills leads to more responsibility and greater independence.

They have no distaste for test taking because they've never taken a test and their learning has not been defined by the subject matter that will appear on the next test. They've discussed the (to them) odd practice of testing children to ascertain what they know and they all agree that if they were faced with such a test they'd give it their best shot but wouldn't be too concerned about the outcome. To our kids failing a test would be much like losing a game — better luck next time around and if it's really important to you you'd better practice up in the meantime!

And yet they don't ignore the need to continually strive for excellence in much of what they do. Our kids are testing themselves all the time in many different ways - testing their abilities and their limits. They hold themselves accountable for their own learning and responsible for each others' learning. They not only quiz each other, asking questions and constantly checking to see what each one knows, but they're also continually helping each other figure things out, put pieces together, sort fact from fiction, and build on their knowledge and experience.

We've always been impressed by their recall abilities. A song or a poem that they like will be memorized after hearing it only a few times. Names of people we've met, towns we've been through, things we've seen or done — they remember it all so much more clearly and easily than we do! We cannot imagine cluttering their phenomenal little minds with dates of the reigns of English kings, or the symbols of the Periodic Table of Elements, if the only reason for knowing these facts is for passing a test of questionable merit. If someday they find a use for the information or an interest in those subjects they'll learn them quickly and much more thoroughly than we could ever hope to teach them!

Our children live in the real world, and their tests are real, not contrived to meet some arbitrary educational guidelines or standards. They test knowledge that is important to them, that is somehow immediately useful or interesting. Reading, spelling, arithmetic, designing and building a new speaker system, changing a recipe to see how it turns out, redesigning their horse's bridle to see if it increases control, endlessly practicing cart wheels and headstands for gymnastics class - these activities are like tests which they design for themselves, meaningful tests which have real significance for them.

And the more we look the more we see that our kids are just like most other kids out there. They are not super kids, we are not super parents and we do not have the super answers. We have found trust in ourselves over trust in test scores.

From the January-February, 1988 issue of *Home Education Magazine.*

The First Step of the Journey

Michelle Delio

Taking the first step onto the path of homeschooling is the hardest part of the journey. Doubts assail you, because the choice to home-school is a decision to set out onto uncharted waters.

These days there are some maps, but as you soon learn, no map drawn by another family will be able to guide you and yours on your own highly personal journey.

At least you have the comfort of knowing that others felt like you do, and you have some pointers as to where to look for provisions and landmarks. At least you do if you're homeschooling younger kids. You're pretty much on your own if your family includes a teenager or two.

A thing I learned a long time ago, and homeschooling reinforced it, is that each family is its own best authority on what its members need. So what I don't propose to do with this column is be a tour guide. I'd rather be the facilitator of an open forum on how we parents of older homeschooled kids are participating in our kid's education. I like the image of all of us setting out on a trip together, pointing out the beautiful scenery on the way, helping each other up the steep hills, and running down the rolling meadows with joy.

To start with, let me tell you a little about our family, so you know who is speaking to you. There are actually three of us, but we are happily part of a large extended family, related either by blood or friendship.

This is our first year of homeschooling, although I've always been interested in the subject. I remember asking my mom, when I was about 14 (15 years ago), if I could stay at home to learn. At that point I had been playing hooky for months and hiding out in the local libraries, where I had developed a reasonably well-rounded reading program for myself. My mom, although she worked for the New York City School Board, was willing to let me try it. But when she investigated the legalities of it she was told that I'd have to be designated as emotionally or physically unable to attend school by a doctor. I don't know if the laws have changed or if she, despite her contacts, just got some bad information. Unwilling to be officially deemed a lunatic, I continued to play hooky until I was able to officially drop out at age

16. I also worked part-time at the Board of Education — enough to turn you off public schooling forever!

When I had my own son, and the magic age arrived at which he was drafted for government service (kindergarten), I seriously considered homeschooling him. But no one was in favor, and my first husband and I were going through some difficult times. So Devon went bravely off to school.

And that's when the problems started. He just wasn't "fitting in". He wasn't unhappy, and had scads of friends, but my bright little son just couldn't get it together enough to do the work. In innumerable teachers conferences I was told that he was immature, that it was because he was an only child, because I was a working mother, because he came from a broken home (I'd gotten a divorce) anything but that their system was at fault. Finally, he was tested for learning disabilities. Lo and behold, they found a "problem" and it was recommended that he be switched to an LD class.

Looking back now I know that Devon's only disability was his refusal to march along with the rest of the good little soldiers that his friends were being trained to become. But I didn't know that then. I breathed a sigh of relief that we'd finally figured out what "the problem" was and now, of course, we could fix it.

But, after three years of watching my son do nothing in school and lose his urge to learn independently ("I can't do that, I have a learning disability" he would say), and watching as the LD classes, which I thought were to be a haven for basically bright kids who couldn't cut it in the overstuffed "regular" classes, became a dumping ground for kids who had massive behavior and emotional problems — and after taking a long and careful look at New York City's Junior High schools (now there's a story Steven King should write) we decided it was either private school or homeschool. After much private thought and family discussion we voted for homeschool.

My first step was to read up on the subject. I consumed books and ordered the entire back issue set of HEM. The magazines were helpful, the books had their moments. The best book about homeschooling older kids is *The Teenage Liberation Handook* by Grace Llewellyn. I also enjoyed *Better Than School* by Nancy Wallace. Although her kids were much younger than mine I began to see a glimmer of the unstructured structure that characterizes our homeschool today.

Because you see, despite all my reading, I still thought my biggest homeschool decision would be what correspondence school to choose.

We sent away for all the brochures and pored over them many nights until early in the morning. Finally we selected the one that seemed the least regimented, and sent several hundred dollars winging their way. Of course, we'd have the advisory teacher service too.

Well, the curriculum arrived and we took a deep breath and plunged in, doing it just as the school said. Being a print oriented family, we supplemented quite heavily with other books. One day I idly asked Devon what he liked about homeschool so far. "I get to read real books — at least sometimes" he said.

That's the moment that we really began to homeschool. Real Books. Of course! How simple. Everything he'd ever need to know we could learn at the library, and the bookstore. We could rent videos, even silly ones like Monty Pythons *Eric The Viking.* We could hang about in museums. We could do whatever we wanted, whatever excited us that day.

Somewhere along the line I discovered what I really believed about education — the most important thing a kid can learn is how to learn. When we first started, I would go to the bookstore and pick out nifty books to supplement whatever we were working on that week. Now we go together and we talk about how to find information on whatever subjects we're studying. We discuss the offshoots of the subject — where else could it take us? We've found out that Vikings can take us into the ocean (science) and along with them on their mythical adventures (Language Arts) and they introduced us to an art filled with intricate swirling figures and motifs (and to reproduce them you need math). And who else was stomping about Europe when the Vikings were terrorizing the coasts? Mongols, Celts, and Huns — all with rich histories and writings and art of their own to explore.

These days, we always have a broad general theme, (ancient history right now) and the various "school" subjects interconnect and flow from each other. Within that theme Devon picks whatever aspect he wants to study. I was a little disconcerted when we did barbarian tribes before Rome and generally messed around with the continuity of history, but again, older kids can understand the abstract idea of the chronology of history, especially with the use of a timeline, so you can do some judicious skipping around without harm. Sometimes this rather blithe approach to history can spark a real interest in a particular time or culture which had been perceived as boring. Devon developed a serious interest in the Barbarian tribes but balked at studying Ancient Rome. Eventually, though, he wanted to know about the great civilization that his beloved Barbarians had so thoroughly trounced, and studied Rome with interest.

Probably the most important thing I've learned this year is that older kids are not quite as sponge-like as the youngsters. The little ones I come into contact with, both homeschooled or not, are less picky about what they'll learn. Older kids have more established likes and dislikes. And believe me, if they're not interested in whatever they're learning, although a polite kid may go through the motions, they're not going to remember it. They'll retain it for just as long as they need to and then it'll be gone. That's why it's so important to let them, as the late Joseph Campbell used to say, "follow their bliss."

Our family has had an amazing year and homeschooling has been the catalyst. Please write and tell us about your family. Let's make this column a resource for all of us who have the privilege and challenge of watching our older kids take charge of their lives and educations.

From the May-June, 1994 issue of *Home Education Magazine.*

Crafting Ships

Mark Hegener

Nine year old Christopher has been working for nearly four hours on his current project. I am not sure how long ago he designed this ship--has it been a process that is years long or is he winging it right now as he drills holes for the rigging and excavates a recessed area in the hull? Ships have always caught his eye and I don't see a new aris-ing passion soon, so the answer is probably both.

At any rate, up to right now it has been four solid hours with three very short breaks. One while he waited for me to help with a couple of quick but fairly tricky saw cuts, another so I could switch bits in the brace he's using, and once when I moved him aside to sweep the wood shavings back into a pile.

I look at the boat he is building and I envision that it is finished out as a three masted bark trimmed to race the Northern Atlantic. Or pos-sibly it will be a sleek sloop outfitted for trade in the South Pacific. Or maybe a cutter to ply the coast of Northern Europe. More than likely it is a hunk of fir that will float the pond on Little Bonaparte Creek, and end up as a flash of light and warmth in an early spring campfire down by the bridge below our dam.

What was his lesson in all of this drilling and sawing and sanding? Was there a lesson for me as well? Who dare put a value on it? There will be no portfolio material produced with this lesson. The project will probably not even rate precious display case status for very long, because there are always so many of these projects and we have many children doing them.

The lessons learned will be carried with Chris alone. Each lesson proving its worth in its own time, from now throughout his lifetime. His life will test his learning, his desire will hone the experience and help him build on what he set out to do. If, many years from now, he chooses to build a full scale vessel, the lessons learned today will be a part of that project. If he never chooses to build a sailing ship the lessons will be there for those other projects as well.

And at the same time he is not alone in this learning. Everyone con-tributes with help, encouragement or suggestions, each drawing on and adding to their own vast store of experiences. I know the tools, the process and I too have studied sailing ships. Younger brother

Michael prowls the perimeter of the project, quick to grab a discarded piece or test an observation or maybe just try out his ability to work a tool. Big sister Jody, knowing little of ships (horses are her passion), searches through material scraps for just the right pieces to make the sails. Mom advises on the kind of needle and thread needed, and the stitching to fashion the sail. Older brother Jim is studying it with the eye of a research engineer. And of course all will offer enthusiastic appreciation when the ship is ready to launch.

Chris has decided that he will let his ship go in the big lake up the road, and he says that it will look good floating off, and that it will probably end up hooked on a branch on the side of the lake or maybe it will drift down the creek, perhaps into the river and eventually out into the ocean. But that launching will have to wait until it is fully rigged and looking real good for its journey. He will know when.

I look a long way past this small boat and whatever ending awaits it. Chris is willing to push this lesson into the great unknown, and I am comfortable with the knowledge that the lessons will last much longer and be much bigger than this lovingly crafted sailing ship.

From the March-April 1991 issue of *Home Education Magazine.*

Of Human Bonds: The Really Right Stuff

Kathleen Creech

I lifted my eyes and looked clear across the library to where Becky sat curled up with a book on the windowseat. She raised her head and met my gaze. We smiled. I pointed at the clock and raised five fingers. She frowned, but nodded before returning to her book.

I found Andy at the blackboard just finishing a panel of Disney characters. I caught his eye and repeated my "five minutes" gesture. He flicked his glance to his drawings, then quickly back to me. The question in his face was obvious. I went to him, hugged him, whispered, "They're some of your best!"

He cupped his hands to my ear. "If only I'd drawn them on paper!"

"Well," I said, "I'm glad I got to see them. Why don't you show them to Becky?"

Andy rushed off to get her while I chatted with my favorite librarian as she checked out our pile of books. Halfway through, I turned and looked toward the blackboard. Andy had his chalk in hand and was shading in Donald's jacket. Becky smiled at me again. Andy saw I was watching and smiled, too.

Three of us, smiling together in the library at... at what? At the funny cartoons Andy had drawn? At his absorption with them? No, we smiled at us... at the good feeling of sharing a private moment in a public world. Time stood still, and I realized that this is one of the intangible benefits of homeschooling: super-bonding.

Bonds need to stretch: elasticity allows growth, yet provides lifelong attachment. Bonds should be just sticky enough to hold through all of life's changes, but not so binding our children can't break free.

"Mom," Andy asked, "Why do they call them rubber bands? Why aren't they rubber bonds? Why have two words that mean the same thing?" He punctuated each question with a snap of the red band stretched between his thumb and forefinger.

"They don't mean the same thing," I asserted, as I reached over and picked up a penny from the floor. Andy steadied his hand while I placed the copper against the rubber band and pulled back. Twang! I let fly. The penny flew through the air and landed on the couch. Andy grinned. He reached in his pocket, extracted a small metal washer and sent it sailing to join my penny. His went farther than mine. I was challenged! I found my own rubber band, and together we searched for objects to hurl at the poor defenseless couch. We said little, we were so intent on our actions. Then the phone rang.

I looked at Andy, and let it ring. I held up my rubber band. "This is a band, and this," I paused and hugged him, "is a bond."

I snatched the received up and said a hasty "Hello!"

"Oh!" A startled voice replied. "I had almost given up! I hope I'm not disturbing anything?"

"No." I looked across the room at Andy who was drawing a bull's eye target on a piece of cereal box. "No, I was just finishing a combination applied physics and language arts lesson."

"Oh, Kathleen! I wish my kids would be interested in those kinds of things!"

I hesitated for one very human moment, then laughed as I 'fessed up to her. "Now that I've set the record straight, what can I do for you, Celia?"

"Well," she cleared her throat. "I just thought you might like to know I am homeschooling two children now!"

"What?!" I cast about for an explanation. "You mean you have taken Hannah out of school, too?"

"Yes!" Celia's precise English accent gave special emphasis to her one-word answer.

I listened to the circumstances surrounding their decision. No two "Reasons why I am homeschooling" stories are the same. Each tale has its own sprinkling of sadness and gladness, tears and cheers.

"Let's get together tomorrow at the swimming pool," she concluded. I put it on the calendar.

We watched our boys and girls swimming and laughing and cannonballing into the deep end of the pool. Celia couldn't take her eyes off her daughter, and I found my own gaze riveted to Celia. I had never seen her so relaxed. Her whole body said, 'I am happy.' She turned and looked at me.

"Do you know what Hannah did? Yesterday she and Nathaniel were sitting at the homeschool table, each of them writing in their story notebooks. I went into the kitchen to make lunch, and when I looked back in on them, I had to laugh! Hannah had made a picture frame out of a big piece of cardboard and placed it over her head. I got the camera and took her picture!"

"She couldn't do that if she were in school!" I said.

"Exactly! That's what I thought! She was still writing on her story, but she had changed her environment to suit herself!"

A dripping Hannah appeared before us. "Mom, I'm going to get out, okay?"

Celia frowned slightly. "All right, but you've only been in a few minutes."

Nine-year-old Hannah shivered and announced, " But I'm cold!"

"Take a hot shower, then, and come sit with me when you're dressed." We watched Hannah drip her way to the locker room.

"The picture frame incident is interesting, Celia, because it's a novel idea for her -- being able to get out of her seat and do something like that without disrupting the class or disobeying the teacher."

Celia smiled, remembering the event. "Yes, she seemed so pleased with herself."

"Is she happy to be home? She's not missing school?" I asked.

"What? Oh! No, not at all!" Celia chuckled, then grew sober. "She does want to see more kids, but not necessarily the ones from school. I don't really know how to tell you what it was like for her in school--and she was a good student, academically. But she's sensitive of others' feelings. Oh, she teases, but she really cares when someone's feelings get hurt. And not just people, but animals. One day the bus-van she rode in to school ran over a squirrel. Do you know that all the kids in the van clapped and cheered?"

I cringed, thinking of how indignant my own would have been if they had been in that van. "Did she get upset?"

Celia grimaced. "Yes! When she told me about it, I was upset!"

"Here, Mom, hold this." Hannah stood beside the bleachers holding out her wet towel and suit.

"Hannah, I don't want to hold that. Put it over there." Hannah did, peered around, spied her mother's unoccupied lap, and climbed on.

In the background, water splashed, kids yelled, and the warm spring sun shone in through the floor to ceiling windows on the south side of the pool. I watched the filtered light change colors in the blue-green waters. I glanced back at Celia, sitting behind me, and up one row. Hannah was curled in her lap, eyes half shut and one thumb warming itself in her mouth. Celia's gaze was on Nathaniel and Andrew, having a race across the pool, but her right hand steadily stroked and smoothed Hannah's long brown hair. Celia saw me, and smiled and hugged Hannah tighter. Hannah squirmed and smiled back.

"It just feels so right," Celia said.

Across the pool, Andy spluttered and wiped water from his face. My boy: until recently the only kid in the pool who could swim and dive and emerge with a dry head! Some things take time, but they feel so right!

From the May-June, 1991 issue of *Home Education Magazine.*

APPENDIX

AUTHOR BIOGRAPHIES

Please note that the biographical information about the writers was current in 1994 and has not been updated for this 2005 edition.

Barker, Penny - Penny Barker wrote a regular column, "In Our Experience," for HEM for several years. Since 1975 Penny and her husband, Richard, have co-directed The Country School, a family centered experience in farmstead living for 6 to 12 year-olds during the summer months, and their family dogsledding business in northern Michigan in the winter. The five Barker children have all been homeschooled.

Brown, Aneeta - Aneeta Brown, a freelance writer living in Leesburg, Virginia, has sold articles to *Family Circle, The Washington Post, Guideposts, Focus on the Family, Writer's Digest, Scholastic Instructor,* and many other publications.

Chodan, Diane - Homeschooling mother Diane Chodan lives in New York state, and her writing has also been published in *Growing Without Schooling.*

Conley, Craig - Craig Conley, a longtime contributor to this publication, lives in Richmond, Virginia. In submitting his music article to HEM, Craig wrote: "I've been interested in the idea of music appreciation for many years. I have interviewed the professor who created Louisiana State University's Music Appreciation course, and much of his philosophy is reflected in this article. In addition, I have written articles about LSU's music library and music listening rooms. If it counts as expertise, I studied the piano for ten years." Craig lives in Murfreesboro, Tennessee.

Creech, Kathleen - Kathleen Creech, author of the popular "Reflections" column in HEM, is mom to Becky (17) and Andy (14). Kathleen is also a member of the online staff for the HEM forum on America Online.

Delio, Michelle - Michelle Delio is a former columnist for HEM. She writes " Our family is composed of one freelance editor and writer (Michelle) an art director (Laszlo) and a video game, comic book and mythology buff (Devon). We also have three black cats who do not care to share their interests with mere humans. We live in New York city, in an apartment filled with new computers, old art, and hundreds of books and magazines." Michelle is also a former member of the online staff for the HEM forum on America Online.

Dobson, Linda - Linda Dobson, the News Watch columnist for HEM, lives in the Adirondack Mountains near Rainbow Lake, New York. A former council member for the National Homeschool Association, Linda's first book, *The Art of Education*, was published by Home Education Press in 1995 (now available from Holt Associates, Cambridge, MA). Linda learns at home with her husband and their children Chuck, Erika, and Adam.

Edwards, Vivienne - Homeschooling mother Vivienne Edwards writes, "For the first time since my children were born I am finding the time to do one of the things I enjoy most - writing. My two girls, now 18 and 20, are all done with homeschooling, so I am hoping to draw on some of our experiences to write about. Vivienne Edwards lives in Harrisburg, Oregon.

Friendlander, Tom - Tom Friendlander has written over fifteen articles for national and regional magazines, and has been actively engaged in the study and promotion of home education in the political and social fields.

Gatto, John Taylor - John Taylor Gatto is an award-winning teacher, including New York City Teacher of the Year for 1989, 1990, and 1991 and New York State Teacher of the Year for 1991. After thirty years of teaching in the public schools, John now travels extensively speaking about education in America. He is the author of *Dumbing Us Down: The Hidden Curriculum of Compulsory Schooling*, and recently edited *The Exhausted School*, which presents several alternatives to the public education system. Both books, plus information about John's workshops and seminars, are available from The Odysseus Group, Inc., 295 E. 8th Street, New York, NY 10023.

Gonet, Lee - Lee and Phil Gonet have been home schooling their two children since birth.. They are co-founders of Alabama Home Educators.

Hegener, Mark and Helen - As editors and publishers of the widely respected homeschooling publication, *Home Education Magazine* (which also supports a popular forum on America Online), Mark and Helen Hegener have been actively and professionally involved with homeschooling since 1983. Their five children (John 22, Jim 20, Jody Ellen 17, Christopher 15, and Michael 10) have all been homeschooled all their lives. The Hegener family lives in Alaska, where they enjoy horsebackriding, gardening, and frequent travels.

Henry, Shari - Shari Henry, a frequent contributor to *Home Education Magazine*, is the homeschooling mother of TJ (9), Bekah (5), and Phoebe (2). She and her husband, Tim Jones, are traveling around the country as his job requires. They currently are living in Bettendorf, Iowa.

Holt, John - John Holt, who died in 1985, was a noted educator and author. He wrote eleven books on education, including *How Children Learn, How Children Fail,* and *Teach Your Own*. In 1977 Holt began publication of the newsletter *Growing*

Without Schooling, which encouraged parents to teach their children at home. John Holt's work is being continued by Holt Associates.

Hummel, Barb - Barb Hummel lives in Berthoud, Colorado.

Leistico, Agnes - The homeschooling mother of three, Agnes Leistico wrote about her family's learning adventures in two widely popular books: *I Learn Better by Teaching Myself* and *Still Teaching Ourselves* (1990 and 1994, originally published by Home Education Press, currently available from Holt Associates, Cambridge, MA). The Leistico family lives near Lompoc, California.

Marcus, Bernard - Bernard Marcus is a Professor of Biology at Genesse Community College in Batavia, New York.

McCarthy, Mary - Long-time homeschooler Mary McCarthy, a frequent contributor to HEM, lives in Westfield, New Jersey.

McCurdy, Kathleen - Kathleen McCurdy, mother of five and a popular homeschooling conference speaker, is Executive Director of the Family Learning Organization, based in Spokane, Washington.

Mitchell-Irwin, Patricia - Patricia Mitchell-Erwin, mother of five sons, is currently working on a degree in Child Development at Murray State University, and plans to do graduate work in Anthropology, concentrating on cross-cultural child rearing, childbirth, and breastfeeding customs. The Mitchell-Erwin family lives in Hazel, Kentucky.

Pagnoni, Mario - Mario Pagnoni is the author of *The Complete Home Educator* (Larson Publications, 1984) and *Computers and Small Fries* (Avery Publishing, 1987).

Pfeil, Connie - Constance Hampton-Pfeil has been involved with homeschooling since her now-13-year-old was 2. None of her three children, Gretchen (age 13), Shawn (age 10), and Sarah (age 1), have ever been to school. Connie co-founded Northern California Homeschool Association and has served as Chairman and as editor of the NCHA News.

Quinn, Sister Catherine - Sister Catherine Quinn, M. Ed., lives in Sherman Oaks, California.

Raymond, Kate - Kate Raymond, a freelance writer and professional craftsperson, lives in Davis, California with her husband Wayne, and children Betsy (5), Nathan (3), and Hope (9 months). She has written reviews for *Northern California Best Places*, articles for *Parents Monthly* and *Parents Corner* and a weekly lifestyle column called *Making*

Ends Meet for the local paper. Currently she and her family make puppets and puppet theaters and sell them at local craft fairs.

Reed, Donn - Author of the popular resource book, *The Home School Source Book*, Donn and his wife Jean live on a fifty-acre homestead in New Brunswick, Canada, about three miles from Maine. They raised and homeschooled three daughters and a son. These days, Jean plays classical guitar and makes doughnuts, while Donn splits wood, milks the cow, and plays with his typewriter. [Donn Reed passed away in late 1995.]

Ressler, Chris - Chris Ressler is the homeschooling mother of Jesse (11), Julie (14), and Seth (17). The Ressler family lives near Redding, California.

Rupp, Becky - Becky Rupp and her husband, Randy, have three sons: Joshua (12), Ethan (10) and Caleb (9) who have always been homeschooled. The Rupp family lives on a small farm near Shaftsbury, Vermont, where Becky works as a freelance writer. Her educational resources book *Good Stuff: Learning Tools for All Ages* (1994, Home Education Press, now available from Holt Associates, Cambridge, MA) won a 1994 Parent's Choice award.

Smith-Heavenrich, Sue - Sue Smith-Heavenrich, a frequent contributor to HEM, is a homeschooling mother and writer. Sue, Lou, and their sons Coulter (7) and Toby (4) live and learn together on a hilltop in Candor, New York. When Sue is not gardening, counting spiders, or writing, she's dreaming up adventures for family outings.

Staten, Robert - Robert Staten is a Special Education teacher in the Albuquerque Public School system. For fifteen years he has taught learning disabled elementary and middle school children in the mountains outside Albuquerque, New Mexico. As Head Teacher for his departments, Mr. Staten has participated in and presided over hundreds of IEP meetings with parents and other teachers. He has written for *New Mexico Magazine*, *The Education Center*, and *Living with Teens*, among others.

Thom, Steve - Homeschooling father Steve Thom lives with his family in Buffalo, Wyoming.

Thompson, Sue - Sue Thompson and her family live in Melbourne, Florida.

Westheimer, Dick and Debbie - Dick and Debbie Westheimer and their children live in Batavia, Ohio, where they are active in their local homeschooling network. Dick is also a council member of the National Homeschool Association, and the Westheimer Family Band records delightful folk-rock music together.

RESOURCES

Books

And the Skylark Sings with Me - Adventures in Homeschooling and Community-Based Education, by David H. Albert. Paperback, 240 pages. (1999) Consortium Book Sales & Dist. ISBN: 0865714010

The Complete Home Learning Source Book: The Essential Resource Guide for Homeschoolers, Parents, and Educators, by Rebecca Rupp. Paperback, 752 pages. (1998) Three Rivers Press. ISBN: 0609801090

Getting Started on Home Learning: How and Why to Teach Your Kids at Home, by Rebecca Rupp. Paperback, 128 pages. (1999) Three Rivers Press. ISBN: 0609803433

Fundamentals of Homeschooling: Notes on Successful Family Living, by Ann Lahrson Fisher. A comprehensive volume designed to encourage and support families who are homeschooling. Publishers' Weekly describes this as a book which "...will remind readers of the benefits of living a life that celebrates the simple things: 'play, conversation, togetherness, and growing up.'" 430 pages, Bibliography, Index, Resources (2002). Nettlepatch Press. ISBN 0-9640813-6-9

Homeschoolers' College Admissions Handbook: Preparing Your 12- to 18-Year-Old for a Smooth Transition, by Cafi Cohen, Linda Dobson (Editor) Paperback - 336 pages (2000) Prima Publishing. ISBN: 0761527540

Homeschooling and the Voyage of Self-Discovery: A Journey of Original Seeking, by David H. Albert. David presents his readers with a collection of gems on topics such as why children are perfectionists, how children learn to read, and the single most important lesson to teach a child. Common Courage Press. ISBN 1-56751-232-1

The Homeschooling Book of Answers: The 88 Most Important Questions Answered by Homeschooling's Most Respected Voices, by Linda Dobson (Editor). Paperback, 384 pages. (1998) Prima Publications. ISBN: 0761513779

Homeschooling Our Children Unschooling Ourselves, by Alison McKee. This compelling story about one family's journey into homeschooling will reassure parents considering homeschooling that nurturing children's natural desire to learn can empower their children to become enthusiastic life-long learners. (2002) Bittersweet House. ISBN 0-96578062-7

Homeschooling The Early Years: Your Complete Guide to Successfully Homeschooling the 3- to 8- Year-Old Child by Linda Dobson, Jamie Miller (Editor). Paperback, 224 pages. (1999) Prima Publications. ISBN: 0761520287

The Home School Source Book by Donn and Jean Reed. Paperback, 480 pages. A veritable smorgasbord of resources, reviews, articles, essays, letters, photos, insights, notes and commentary about a wide selection of learning materials. (2005) Brook Farm Books. ISBN 0-919761-28-3

Taking Charge Thru Homeschooling: Personal and Political Empowerment, by Larry & Susan Kaseman. A comprehensive guidebook examining the social and political implications of homeschooling and the potential effect on individual families; recommended for anyone interested in the dynamics and the politics of the homeschooling movement. Solid, practical advice. 288 pages, indexed, resources (1990) Koshkonong Press. ISBN 0-9628365-0-8.

Recommended Resources

American Homeschool Association
http://americanhomeschoolassociation.org
A free services organization which works primarily online to provide information, and support for homeschooling families, education officials, the media and others interested in homeschooling.

Ann Zeise's A to Z Homeschooling
http://gomilpitas.com/homeschooling
A large and multi-faceted website offering friendly encouragement and helpful assistance from a dedicated homeschooling mom.

Home Education Magazine
PO Box 1083
Tonasket, WA 98855
(509) 486-1351
email Info@homeedmag.com
http://www.homeedmag.com
Visit the Home Education Magazine web site for a free sample magazine, free downloadable Homeschooling Information and Resource Guide, free articles to read online, plus free access to newsletters, discussion lists, weblogs, resources and much more!

National Home Education Network
http://www.nhen.org
A national organization for homeschooling families, offering a collection of services and resources. Free membership, media outreach and public relations programs.

Unschooling.com
http://www.unschooling.com
A full-service website designed specifically for unschoolers, offering free weblogs, a library of articles and essays on unschooling, an email discussion list, extensive unschooling resources and much more.

INDEX

For Additional Copies:

The Homeschool Reader: Collected Articles from Home Education Magazine, 1984-1994, Third Revised Edition, is available for $17.95 from Home Education Magazine, PO Box 1083, Tonasket, WA 98855; (800) 236-3278. www.thehomeschoolreader.com

Shipping: Please add $4.25 shipping and handling. Or order through your favorite bookstore.

This book is available at quantity discounts for bulk purchases. For information and rates on bulk purchase and wholesale orders contact: wholesale@thehomeschoolreader.com http://thehomeschoolreader.com

For a free sample issue of *Home Education Magazine* write to Home Education Magazine, PO Box 1083, Tonasket, WA 98855-1083; (800) 236-3278; Orders@homeedmag.com; www.homeedmag.com

Printed in the United States
102407LV00004B/40-42/A